GEOMETRIC
GRAPHICS
A VISUAL CELEBRATION OF SIMPLE FORMS

ISBN 978-1-58423-577-4

First Published in the United States of America by
Gingko Press by arrangement with
Sandu Publishing Co., Ltd.

Text edited by Gingko Press.

Gingko Press, Inc.
1321 Fifth Street
Berkeley, CA 94710 USA
Tel: (510) 898 1195
Fax: (510) 898 1196
Email: books@gingkopress.com
www.gingkopress.com

Copyright © 2014 by Sandu Publishing
First published in 2014 by Sandu Publishing

Sponsored by Design 360°
– Concept and Design Magazine

Edited and produced by
Sandu Publishing Co., Ltd.

Book design, concepts & art direction by
Sandu Publishing Co., Ltd.
Chief Editor: Wang Shaoqiang

Cover inspired by the project of Anne Hellman Vold

info@sandupublishing.com
www.sandupublishing.com

Printed and bound in China

CONTENTS

006 Preface
008 Imprimerie DC
012 La Transat Ag2r La Mondiale
016 Doctor Manzana
020 1-2-3-Helsinki! Design en Seine
024 HEYPETETONG Branding
026 Geome3
028 Timeless Fitness
032 Fresh Tracks Europe
036 MCP – Educación Medioambiental 2012-2013
038 Midlight
040 Mobile M+ Yau Ma Tei Exhibition
044 Dock M
046 Locomotiva
048 Katowice Street Art Festival
052 CIRCOLE
056 Kixbox SS/13
060 Formes Simples
062 Other Press Brand Identity
066 Context: Un Band per Genova
068 Red Room
070 Multinational Typeface
074 Voyage
076 NLRF2013
078 MeteoPoem
080 Raumwelten
084 Meteor Project: A Poster Series
086 Typefaces
088 Tribeca Film Festival Poster Series
090 Så dansade Zarathustra
092 Album Anatomy
096 The Transcontinental Express
098 German Haus
102 CIN | Goethe Institute
104 9th Anniversary of Sala Pasternak
106 Centre Culturel Itinérant France / Pays-Bas
110 Lamber Identity
111 Artfad 2013
112 MCP – Educación Medioambiental 2013-2014
114 LCC—Summer Show Branding and Design
118 Identity of the Museum of Contemporary Art in Buenos Aires
122 Fresh Tracks Europe - Innovation in Dance for Young Audiences
124 Genova City Logo
128 Herschel Supply Studio – Catalog & Seasonal Branding
130 2014 Utzon Music Series Identity
132 Origine Art
134 Bruken Brochure From B to N

136 The Floor
138 H2 Rebranding
140 Galactic Structure
142 Degree Show 2013 Invitation Pack
144 Agenda CCCB 2013
145 BAUHAUS Leistung
146 Formex, Nordic Charm
148 Agulha
150 Shifting Frames
152 Formex – Eclectic Touch
153 Agenda CCCB 2012
154 SOT Branding
158 0.0 Online Marketing
162 London Bar
164 Framework Design Elements
166 Johnny Johnson Identity
167 Name Card
168 Nakato
169 Branding Project for Roma Editora
170 CRUX
172 Geometry Pastas
174 Nördik Impakt 15
178 Bergen International Festival
182 Fashion Walk Fashion Destination
184 AOO
188 Rítmia. Music Therapy
192 Cryptographer & Encoded Textiles
194 Residency Branding
198 3D
202 Book, Publishing House
204 Neurotrend
206 Music Museum of Barcelona
208 Hotel FOMF
210 Delafé y las Flores Azules
211 Brighton Road Studios
212 Má da Fita Identity
214 Tin Can
218 Evo – Back to Basics
220 Geometreek
222 Little Prince Museum Visual Identity
226 Match Exhibition
228 Gold Foiled Notebooks
230 Ambiência
232 UNSW 60th Anniversary Identity
233 Tees Linotype
234 Index
240 Acknowledgments

PREFACE

Graphic design is a little bit like life itself. We must adapt, edit and apply flexibility when working on building brands and working within the arena of graphic design. Graphic design works not only for the present, but the future, and thus should work in 5, 10 or 15 years time. Just as our cultural intake within society constantly morphs, so to, should the language we use to communicate. Graphic design, in this context, is no longer about creating "logos"; from a designer's viewpoint, it is, and should be, a response to such evolutions.

The outstanding and progressive work contained within **Geometric Graphics** shows a true understanding of the aforementioned, utilizing geometric forms and structures applied to branding and graphic design which adapts, morphs and changes throughout various applications.

Systems of communication that change and adapt must be part of the evolution of graphic design and branding. This will maintain cohesion but allow progression and longevity. It will bring structure to form design and brand awareness.

The work contained within **Geometric Graphics** has a timeless flexibility, a simplicity of form and elegance. Much of it is work which can clearly be traced back to some of the great refined styles at two design schools in Switzerland, one in Basel led by Armin Hofmann and Emil Ruder, and the other in Zurich under the leadership of Joseph Muller-Brockmann. These greats of graphic design studied with Ernst Keller at the Zurich School of Design before WWII, where the principles of the Bauhaus and Jan Tschichold's New Typography were taught.

The featured work shows bold, brave and experimental graphic design at its very best — many of the projects contained within the pages to come show a true appreciation for craft, allowing time to process and develop the ideas to make sure the final result and execution is as strong as the process and ideals behind it. This can, and should, apply to any area within graphic design, and not solely with the use of geometric based graphic design.

One of the stand-out projects in **Geometric Graphics** is by multi-award winning Studio Dumbar of the Netherlands — one of my favorite design studios at present. This project, as many others do, shows as an innate sensibility at handling "back to basics" shapes, geometric graphics, and colors and execution, which are beautifully balanced with crisp, clean and modern typography. We see a simplicity in its ultimate form and contemporary graphic design that is backed by the classic and timeless Swiss design principles. The project "La Transat" by Rejane Dal Bello, a former designer at Studio Dumbar, highlights this approach to graphic design, where-by the visual language can adapt through progression and evolve over time to create truly inspirational and timeless work. The geometric shapes combined with bold use of colors and overlaying imagery give this project a fresh, dynamic, and progressive feel, but above all show the flexibility of a clever system which can work and adapt through many forms of communication.

Systems that balance flexibility with purist graphic design tendencies, resulting in flawless execution, are fruitful throughout this book. Classic yet timeless. Swiss design sensibilities and ideals. Modernist aesthetics balanced by bold and "back to basics" graphic design which mirrors our role as designers in the ever changing cultural landscape of communication of language and design. Most notably, these processes of modernism in the graphic design approach tend to lead with experiments in geometric forms and structures. Some commentators define modernism as "a socially progressive trend of thought that affirms the power of human beings to create, improve and reshape their environment with the aid of practical experimentation, or technology."

I couldn't agree more. In this context, **Geometric Graphics** and the great modernist inspired graphic design presented in this book show just that; they are a breath of progressive fresh air, timeless ideas morphed into the new.

"To complicate is easy, to simplify is hard. To complicate, just add, everyone is able to complicate. Few are able to simplify." — Bruno Munari.

Pete Rossi
Founder of RM&CO

IMPRIMERIE DC

The general concept was designed to be clean, bright, and beautiful. Charles Daoud aimed to show that print could still look cool and flashy if done right, despite being a medium viewed as being slowly on the decline. To accomplish this goal, Charles Daoud opted for a dynamic identity system based on geometry and Pop Art that would engage the end user in a rich, fun environment. They developed a full inventory of printed collateral and promotional items, including a reversible cubic calendar, a goodie box, full stationery, and much more.

Creative & Art Direction: Charles Daoud ***Design:*** Charles Daoud, Stefanie René & Kim Peters

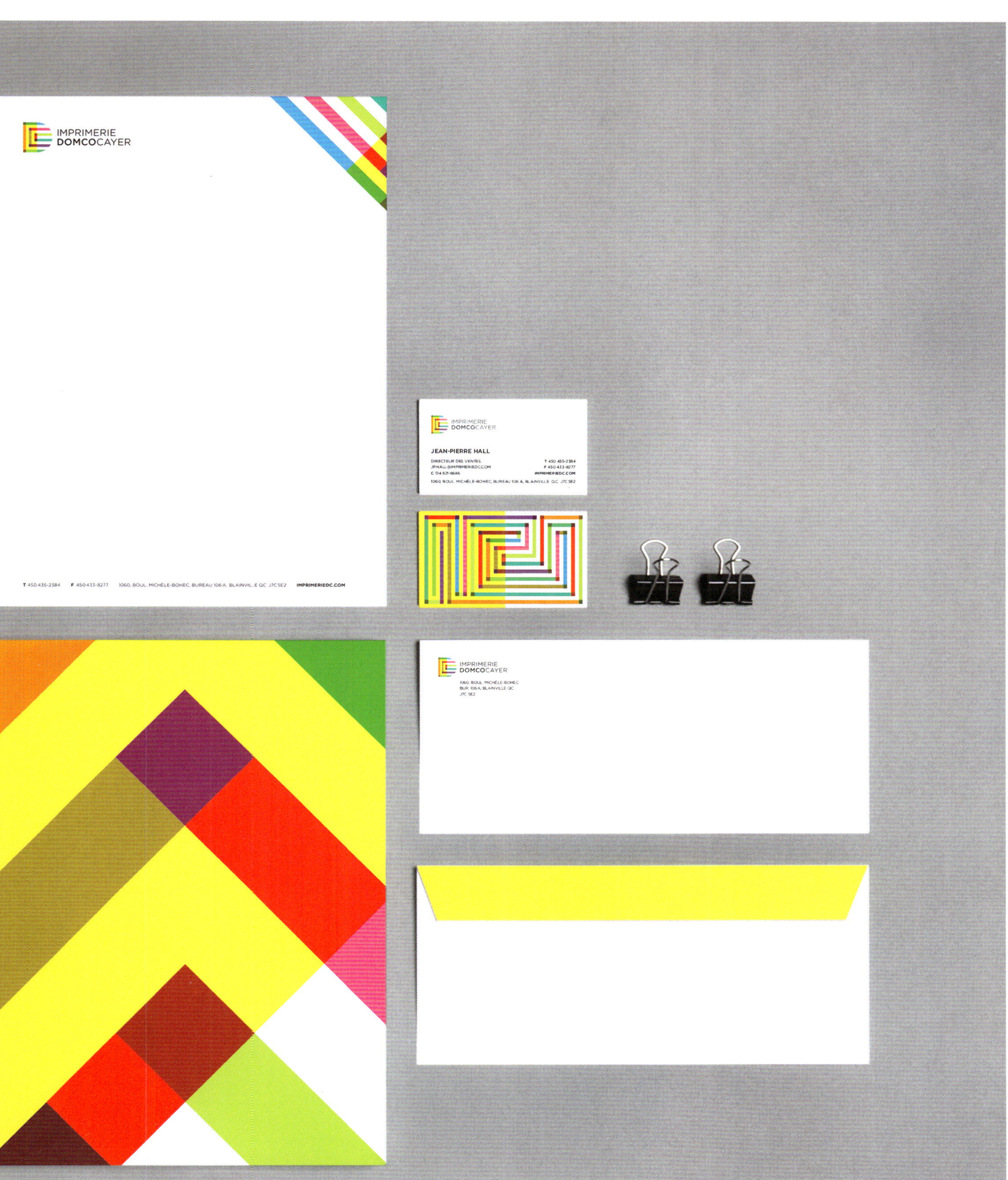

LA TRANSAT AG2R LA MONDIALE

Visual identity Ag2r La Mondiale. This new style was launched in Paris with an extensive campaign that included 125 posters measuring up to 4 x 3 meters. The design is a further evolution of the visual identity that Rejane Dal Bello designed at Studio Dumbar for the French insurance company.

Design: Rejane Dal Bello

AG2R LA MONDIALE
TRANSAT 20 ANS
CONCARNEAU — SAINT-BARTH
DÉPART 21 AVRIL 2012

TRANSAT 20 ANS
CONCARNEAU — SAINT-BARTH
DÉPART 21 AVRIL 2012

AG2R LA MONDIALE
CONCARNEAU — SAINT-BARTH
DÉPART 21 AVRIL 2012
TRANSAT 20 ANS

DOCTOR MANZANA

Masquespacio presents their latest project realized for Doctor Manzana, a store specializing in technical services for smart phones and tablets, as well as a seller of design gadgets for mobile devices. The project reflects the redesign of Doctor Manzana's branding and the realization of the design for their first point of sale located in Valencia, Spain.

Design Agency: Masquespacio **Design:** Ana Milena Hernández Palacios **Photography:** David Rodríguez **Client:** Doctor Manzana

Doctor
Manzana

Doctor
Manzana

¿Es un
traum
¡NO!
Es un equipo de técnicos
especialistas en golpes,
caídas y atropellos de
Smartphones y Tablets

1-2-3-HELSINKI! DESIGN EN SEINE

From May 31st to June 4th 2012 the Finnish Institute in Paris presented 1–2–3–Helsinki! Design en Seine, a unique pop-up event in Paris. The event was an official satellite event of World Design Capital Helsinki 2012.
The event took place during a city-wide design festival called Designer's Days. Two small villages of shipping containers were built on the riverbanks of the Seine, located at the Port de la Tournelle in the immediate vicinity of the Notre Dame cathedral, and the Port de la Gare.

Design Agency: Werklig

1-2-3-HELSINKI!
DESIGN en SEINE

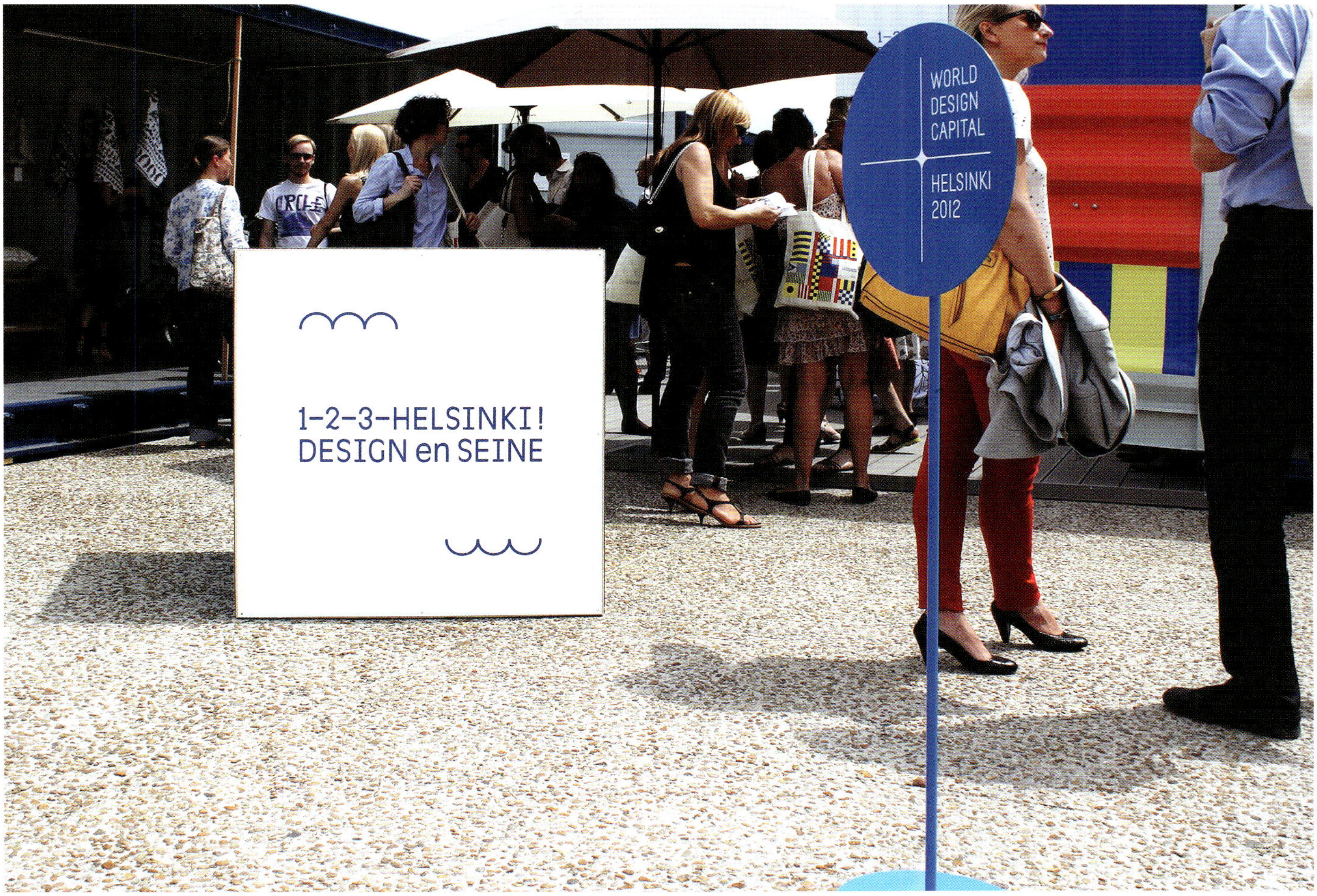

1-2-3-HELSINKI!
DESIGN en SEINE
WORLD
DESIGN
CAPITAL
HELSINKI
2012

HEYPETETONG BRANDING

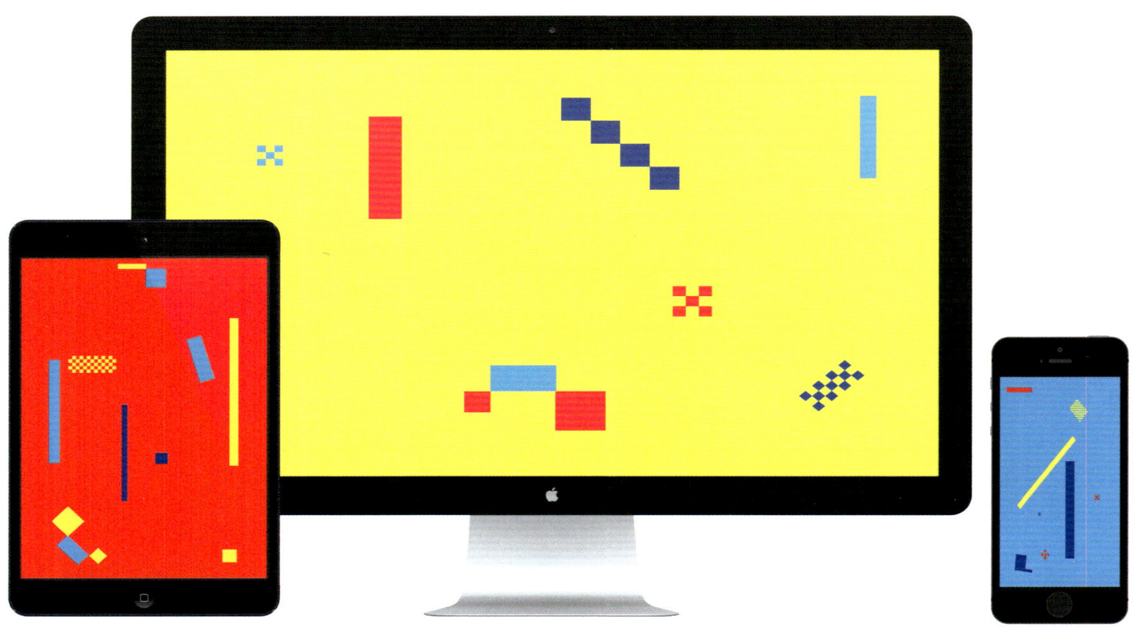

HEYPETETONG is a personal branding project. The color bars of a television test screen that were the inspiration for the project were translated and applied across the studio's branding materials. A partial speech bubble represents the effective communication between the studio and clients.

Design: Pete Tong

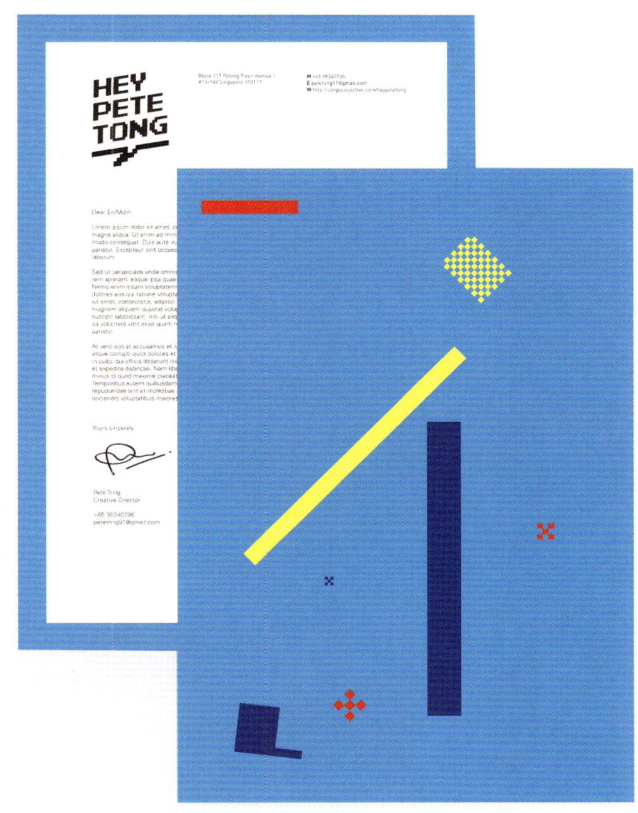

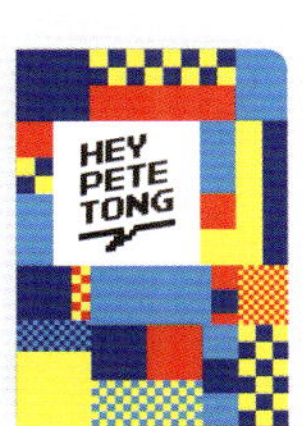

GEOME3

At Geome3, Applove does its utmost to provide attractive, well-designed products.
All cases are flexible and engineered with a soft-touch coating to please even the most discriminating palm, as well as ensuring slippage-free interaction when using the phone above abysses, shark-infested waters, wet cement or lava. All cases are designed to protect the device without interfering with any of its functions.

Design Agency: Applove *Creative Direction:* Applove *Photography:* Fredrik Skogkvist

TIMELESS FITNESS

For one evening, the creative agency Karl Anders devoted their time towards critical thinking about the modern concept of time, while immersing themselves in an entertaining environment. The goal was to create an outstanding identity for this evening called "Timeless Fitness." It was simultaneously an event, a party, a happening, and a performance evening. The project included the implementation of fliers, posters, and online communication.

Design: Marcel Häusler *Text:* Regina Pichler

Unbedingt
LESEN:
WEIL KEINER ZEIT HAT,
HALTEN WIR UNS
KURZ: WIR LADEN SIE
EIN. UND FALLEN DABEI
GEMEINSAM IN EINE
NEUE ZEIT. ZUM FEST-
HALTEN GIBT ES
DRINKS, ZUM AUF-
FALLEN TANZBARE
MUSIK. UND DIE
EINMALIGE MÖGLICH-
KEIT, AKTIV MIT DER
ZEIT ZU GEHEN.
DRESSCODE: ZEITLOS
Da Zeit Geld ist,
bitte schnell hier
anmelden:
zirkel@karlanders.de
Go. Go. Go.
Karl Anders

präsentiert
»Der Zirkel, der macht«
»Der Zirkel, der macht«
»Der Zirkel, der macht«
DO
14. 11. 13
21.00h
IT'S A PARTY
TIMELESS FITNESS
Brunnen
hofstr. 2
HH

TIMELESS FITNESS
»Der Zirkel, der macht«
»Der Zirkel, der macht«
»Der Zirkel, der macht«
DO 14.11.13 AB 21.00 UHR
Brunnen hofstr. 2 HH
PRÄSENTIERT
FYI: IT'S A PARTY
GO. GO. GO.
THE BRAIN RUNS ON FUN.
Karl Anders
Büro für Visual Stories

FRESH TRACKS EUROPE

Fresh Tracks Europe is a youth dance network for a new generation of choreographers. Their new identity is based on a set of dancing body parts and colored shapes. With these building blocks Trapped in Suburbia created an identity symbolizing the philosophy of Fresh Tracks Europe, where the different European dance groups work together to create a new dance generation. There are two directions to the identity, which consists of logos, colors, animations, stationary, business cards, posters, flyers, banners, leaflets, and the website.

Design Agency: Trapped in Suburbia ***Creative Direction:*** Cuby Gerards & Karin Langeveld ***Design:*** Cuby Gerards, Karin Langeveld & Sebastian Pataki

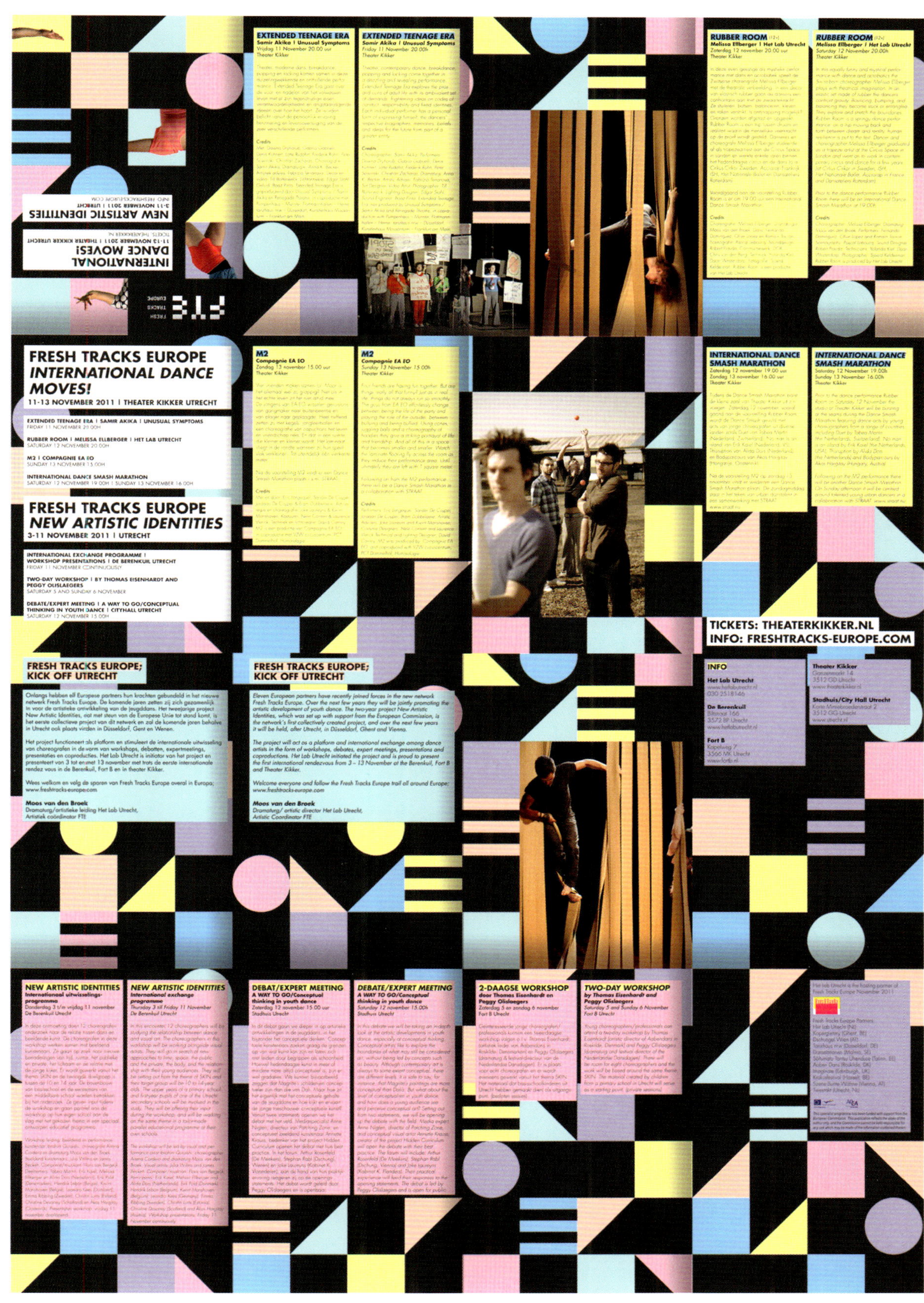

EXTENDED TEENAGE ERA
Samir Akika | Unusual Symptoms
Vrijdag 11 November 20.00 uur
Theater Kikker

EXTENDED TEENAGE ERA
Samir Akika | Unusual Symptoms
Friday 11 November 20.00h
Theater Kikker

RUBBER ROOM (12+)
Melissa Ellberger | Het Lab Utrecht
Zaterdag 12 november 20.00 uur
Theater Kikker

RUBBER ROOM (12+)
Melissa Ellberger | Het Lab Utrecht
Saturday 12 November 20.00h
Theater Kikker

NEW ARTISTIC IDENTITIES
3-11 NOVEMBER 2011 | UTRECHT

INTERNATIONAL DANCE MOVES!
11-13 NOVEMBER 2011 | THEATER KIKKER UTRECHT
TICKETS: THEATERKIKKER.NL
INFO: FRESHTRACKS-EUROPE.COM

FTE FRESH TRACKS EUROPE

FRESH TRACKS EUROPE
INTERNATIONAL DANCE MOVES!
11-13 NOVEMBER 2011 | THEATER KIKKER UTRECHT

EXTENDED TEENAGE ERA | SAMIR AKIKA | UNUSUAL SYMPTOMS
FRIDAY 11 NOVEMBER 20.00H

RUBBER ROOM | MELISSA ELLBERGER | HET LAB UTRECHT
SATURDAY 12 NOVEMBER 20.00H

M2 | COMPAGNIE EA EO
SUNDAY 13 NOVEMBER 15.00H

INTERNATIONAL DANCE SMASH MARATHON
SATURDAY 12 NOVEMBER 19.00H | SUNDAY 13 NOVEMBER 16.00H

FRESH TRACKS EUROPE
NEW ARTISTIC IDENTITIES
3-11 NOVEMBER 2011 | UTRECHT

INTERNATIONAL EXCHANGE PROGRAMME |
WORKSHOP PRESENTATIONS | DE BERENKUIL UTRECHT
FRIDAY 11 NOVEMBER CONTINUOUSLY

TWO-DAY WORKSHOP | BY THOMAS EISENHARDT AND
PEGGY OLISLAEGERS
SATURDAY 5 AND SUNDAY 6 NOVEMBER

DEBATE/EXPERT MEETING | A WAY TO GO/CONCEPTUAL
THINKING IN YOUTH DANCE | CITYHALL UTRECHT
SATURDAY 12 NOVEMBER 15.00H

M2
Compagnie EA EO
Zondag 13 november 15.00 uur
Theater Kikker

M2
Compagnie EA EO
Sunday 13 November 15.00h
Theater Kikker

INTERNATIONAL DANCE SMASH MARATHON
Zaterdag 12 november 19.00 uur
Zondag 13 November 16.00 uur
Theater Kikker

INTERNATIONAL DANCE SMASH MARATHON
Saturday 12 November 19.00h
Sunday 13 November 16.00h
Theater Kikker

TICKETS: THEATERKIKKER.NL
INFO: FRESHTRACKS-EUROPE.COM

FRESH TRACKS EUROPE;
KICK OFF UTRECHT

Onlangs hebben elf Europese partners hun krachten gebundeld in het nieuwe netwerk Fresh Tracks Europe. De komende jaren zetten zij zich gezamenlijk in voor de artistieke ontwikkeling van de jeugddans. Het tweejarige project New Artistic Identities, dat met steun van de Europese Unie tot stand komt, is het eerste collectieve project van dit netwerk en zal de komende jaren behalve in Utrecht ook plaats vinden in Düsseldorf, Gent en Wenen.

Moos van den Broek
Dramaturg/artistieke leiding Het Lab Utrecht,
Artistiek coördinator FTE

FRESH TRACKS EUROPE;
KICK OFF UTRECHT

Eleven European partners have recently joined forces in the new network Fresh Tracks Europe. Over the next few years they will be jointly promoting the artistic development of youth dance. The two-year project New Artistic Identities, which was set up with support from the European Commission, is the network's first collectively created project, and over the next few years it will be held, after Utrecht, in Düsseldorf, Ghent and Vienna.

Moos van den Broek
Dramaturg/ artistic director Het Lab Utrecht,
Artistic Coordinator FTE

INFO

Het Lab Utrecht
De Berenkuil
Fort B

Theater Kikker
Stadhuis/City Hall Utrecht

NEW ARTISTIC IDENTITIES
International uitwisselings-programma
Donderdag 3 t/m vrijdag 11 november
De Berenkuil Utrecht

NEW ARTISTIC IDENTITIES
International exchange programme
Thursday 3 till Friday 11 November
De Berenkuil Utrecht

DEBAT/EXPERT MEETING
A WAY TO GO/Conceptual thinking in youth dance
Zaterdag 12 November 15.00 uur
Stadhuis Utrecht

DEBATE/EXPERT MEETING
A WAY TO GO/Conceptual thinking in youth dance
Saturday 12 November 15.00h
Stadhuis Utrecht

2-DAAGSE WORKSHOP
door Thomas Eisenhardt en Peggy Olislaegers
Zaterdag 5 en zondag 6 november
Fort B Utrecht

TWO-DAY WORKSHOP
by Thomas Eisenhardt and Peggy Olislaegers
Saturday 5 and Sunday 6 November
Fort B Utrecht

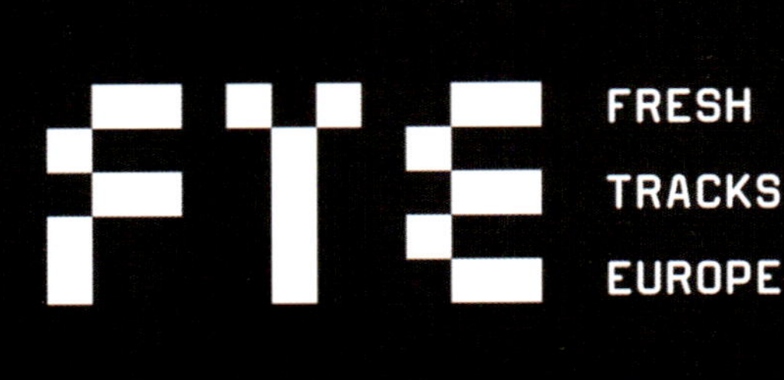
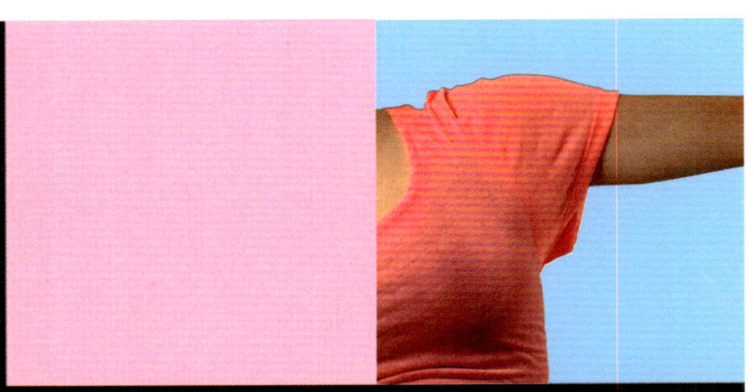
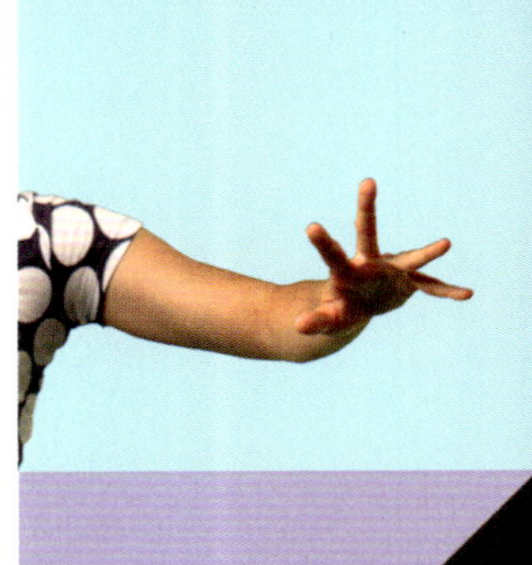

FTE
FRESH
TRACKS
EUROPE

INTERNATIONAL
DANCE MOVES!
11-13 NOVEMBER
THEATER KIKKER UTRECHT | WWW.THEATERKIKKER.NL

VR 11 NOV | 20.00 UUR
EXTENDED TEENAGE ERA
SAMIR AKIKA | UNUSUAL SYMPTOMS

ZA 12 NOV | 20.00 UUR
RUBBER ROOM
MELISSA ELLBERGER | HET LAB UTRECHT

ZO 13 NOV | 15.00 UUR
M2
COMPAGNIE EA EO

ZA 12 NOV 19.00 UUR | ZO 13 NOV 16.00 UUR
INTERNATIONALE DANCE
SMASH MARATHON

WWW.FRESHTRACKS-EUROPE.COM

FTE
FRESH TRACKS EUROPE
INTERNATIONAL DANCE MOVES!
11-13 NOVEMBER
THEATER KIKKER UTRECHT | WWW.THEATERKIKKER.NL
EXTENDED TEENAGE ERA
RUBBER ROOM
M2
INTERNATIONALE DANCE SMASH MARATHON

FTE
FRESH TRACKS EUROPE
FRESHTRACKS-EUROPE.COM
FTE
FRESH TRACKS EUROPE
FRESHTRACKS-EUROPE.COM

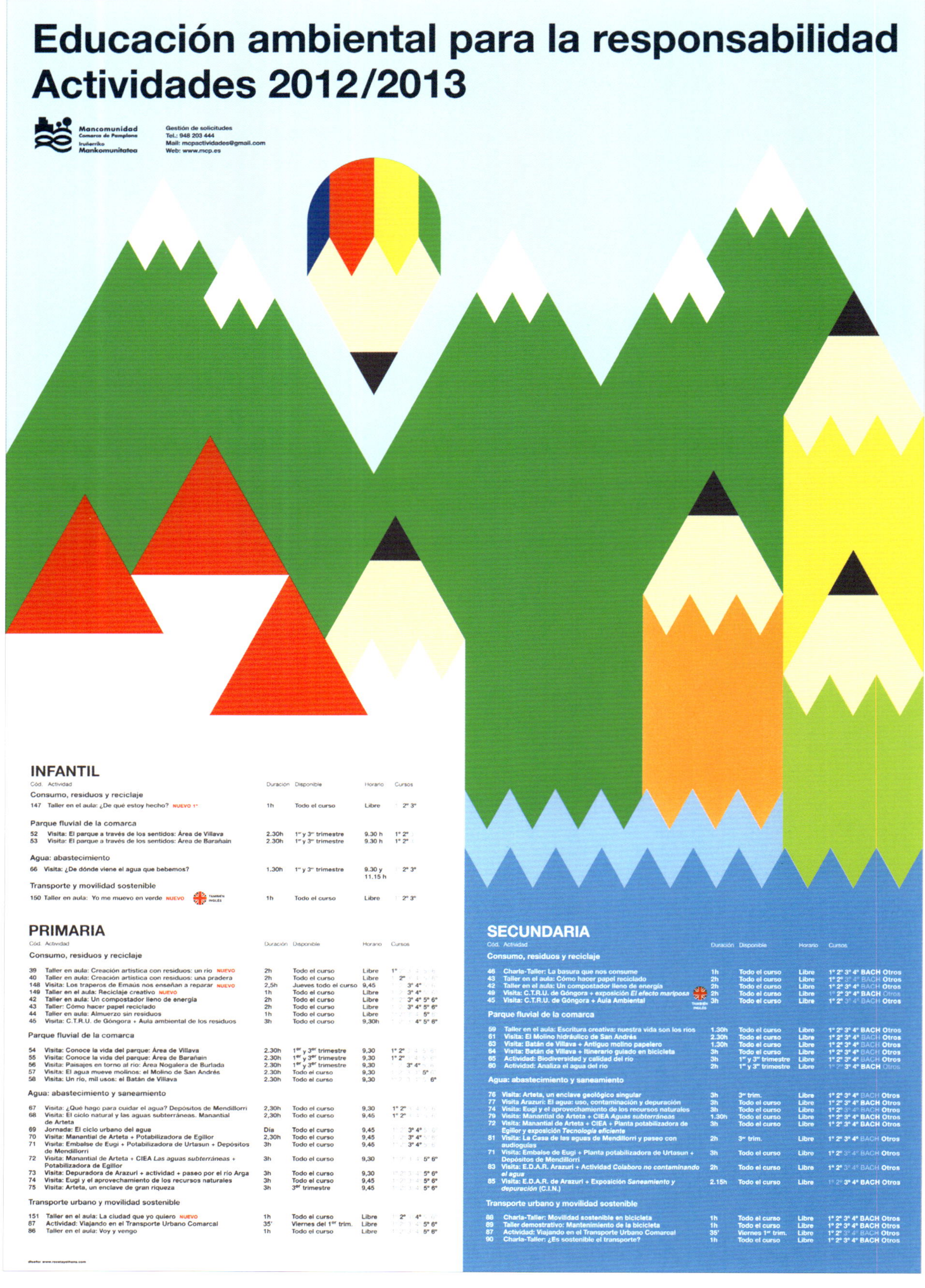

In the 2012-2013 edition of "Educación Medioambiental" brochures, Roseta y Oihana designed a simple yet friendly and witty way to distinguish the different activities available at the event. The pencil was chosen as one of the best representations of learning, and its triangular and squared shapes were used to create illustrations that represented the environment, specifically the water, mountains, and city that were depicted on the covers of the programs. For the event posters, they created a landscape using the same elements used in the brochure covers.

Design Agency: Roseta y Oihana **Illustration:** Oihana Herrera Erneta

SECUNDARIA
Educación ambiental para la responsabilidad
Actividades 2012/2013
Mancomunidad
Comarca de Pamplona
Iruñerriko
Mankomunitatea

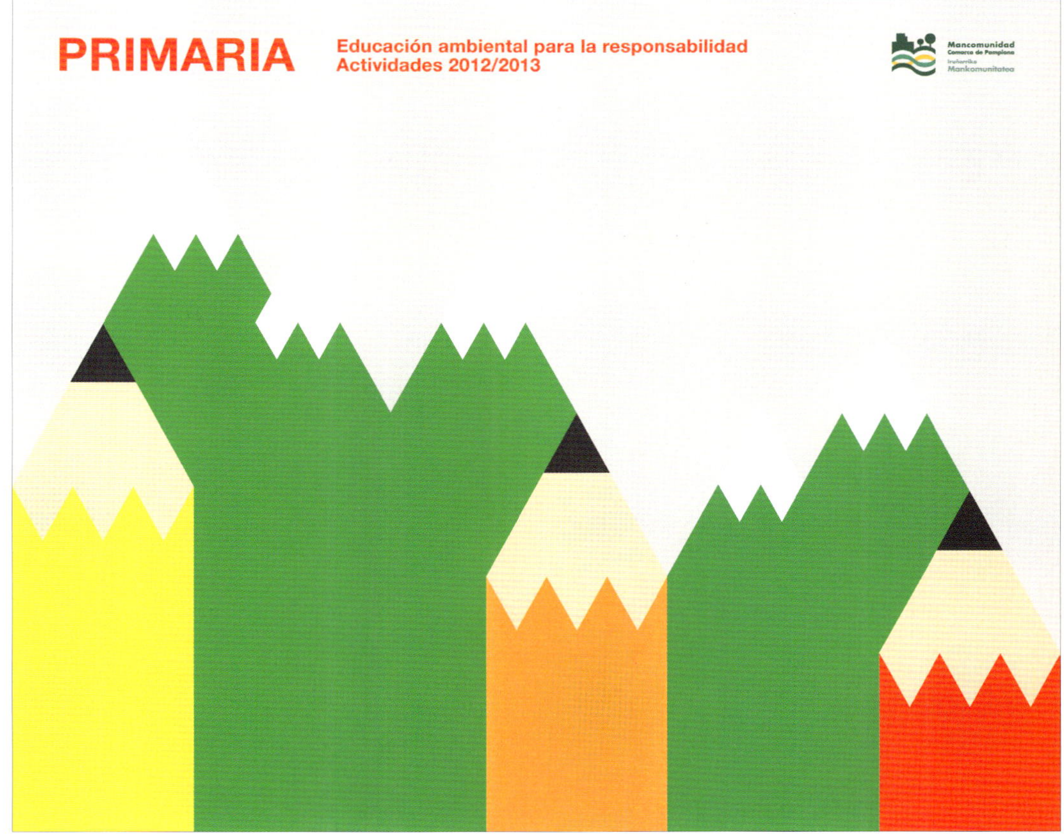

PRIMARIA
Educación ambiental para la responsabilidad
Actividades 2012/2013
Mancomunidad
Comarca de Pamplona
Iruñerriko
Mankomunitatea

MIDLIGHT

Midlight is all about sharing and supporting love for the deeper, more raw sides of electronic music. They work with live musicians, DJs with a taste for organic sounds, passionate believers, and sculptural and visual artists. Studio Naam creates new graphics for every edition to reach Midlight's audience.

Design Agency: Studio Naam ***Creative Direction:*** Timothy Maurer

Midlight proudly presents
the sickest parties in town.
It's your chance to become
one of us and check out
this sick new party:

MIDLIGHT AREA #01

► **DJ SOTOFETT
(SEX TAGS MANIA)
// 5H SET!**

DICKIE ROSEWATER

MIDLIGHT AREA #02

**PAUL DU LAC
(BIO RHYTM, CLONE)**

**JOE MANISH
AND JORGE SPENCER
// B2B**

ARIE GHETTO

OBERMAN

More information about
Midlight can be found at
www.midlight.nl

This is an official Midlight
mediacast.

Doors open:

MOBILE M+ YAU MA TEI EXHIBITION

M+ is the new museum for visual culture in Hong Kong. Mobile M+: Yau Ma Tei, as the first of a series of contemporary art exhibitions, presents six large art installations challenging the layered narratives of the city. The visual identity of the exhibition's promotional items was designed by TGIF. A variety of positive and negative forms are used to represent the close relationship of the artists and the local community that is at the core of "Mobile M+: Yau Ma Tei," the main purpose of which is to bring the concepts of art and museums into society. Simple forms are used to make a contemporary visual impact in the crowded area.

Design Agency: TGIF

MOBILE
進行
YAU MA TEI 油麻地
15.5-10.6.2012

M+ is the new museum for visual culture in Hong Kong. Mobile M+ : Yau Ma Tei, as the first of a series of exhibitions, presents six large art installations, challenging the layered narratives of our city.

PARTICIPATING ARTISTS
Pak Sheung-chuen
Kwan Sheung-chi & Wong Wai-yin
Tsang Kin-wah
Erkka Nissinen
Leung Mee-ping
Yu Lik-wai

Presented by West Kowloon Cultural District Authority
www.wkcda.hk/mobile-mplus

19 MAY 2012
ASIA ART ARCHIVE
BACKROOM CONVERSATIONS
FOR ART HK 12

余力為 Yu Lik-wai
FANTOMAS

MOBILE
進行
YAU MA TEI 油麻地
15.5-10.6.2012

MOBILE M+
進行
YAU MA TEI 油麻地
15.5–10.6.2012
西九文化區管理局主辦
當代藝術展
A contemporary art exhibition
presented by West Kowloon
Cultural District Authority
www.wkcda.hk/mobile-mplus

MOBILE M+
進行
YAU MA TEI 油麻地
15.5–10.6.2012
西九文化區管理局主辦
當代藝術展
A contemporary art exhibition
presented by West Kowloon
Cultural District Authority
www.wkcda.hk/mobile-mplus

MOBILE M+
進行
15.5–10.6.2012

DOCK M

Identity system for a beach bar in Mörbisch, Austria.

Design: Alexander Egger

DOCK M
strandbar

DOCK M strandbar
dock-m.at
DOCK M strandbar
dock-m.at

LOCOMOTIVA

The idea of Locomotiva was constructed through the use of pre-existing and easily recognizable images. It was subsequently a process of visual interpretation and a simplification of forms, where simplified elements were placed in constant repetition but also framed in unexpected contexts.

Design: Inês Castro

21DESIGNERS

KATOWICE STREET ART FESITIVAL

Dynamic, diversity, originality, manifesto – these are the key words used by the organizers of the 3rd Katowice Street Art Festival to describe street art. The visual identity was designed to express the collision between the often conflicting energies contained in street art and their liberation during the festival.

Design: Marta Gawin **Client:** Instytucja Kultury Katowice Miasto Ogrodów

Katowice
Street Art
Festival
19—28 IV
2013 r.

Instytucja Kultury
Katowice
— Miasto Ogrodów
zaprasza
Katowice
Street Art
Festival
19—28 IV
2013 r.
murale
instalacje
wystawy
muzyka
warsztaty
filmy
debata
katowicestreetartfestival.pl
facebook.com/KatowiceStreetArtFestival
miasto-ogrodow.eu

Instytucja Kultury
Katowice
— Miasto Ogrodów
zaprasza
Katowice
Street Art
Festival
19—28 IV
2013 r.
murale
instalacje
wystawy
muzyka
warsztaty
filmy
debata
katowicestreetartfestival.pl
facebook.com/KatowiceStreetArtFestival
miasto-ogrodow.eu

Instytucja Kultury
Katowice
— Miasto Ogrodów
zaprasza
Katowice
Street Art
Festival
19—28 IV
2013 r.
murale
instalacje
wystawy
muzyka
warsztaty
filmy
debata
katowicestreetartfestival.pl
facebook.com/KatowiceStreetArtFestival
miasto-ogrodow.eu

Instytucja Kultury
Katowice
— Miasto Ogrodów
zaprasza
Katowice
Street Art
Festival
19—28 IV
2013 r.
murale
instalacje
wystawy
muzyka
warsztaty
filmy
debata
katowicestreetartfestival.pl
facebook.com/KatowiceStreetArtFestival
miasto-ogrodow.eu

Katowice
Street Art
Festival
19—28 IV
2013 r.
murale
instalacje
wystawy
muzyka
warsztaty
filmy
debata

CIRCOLE

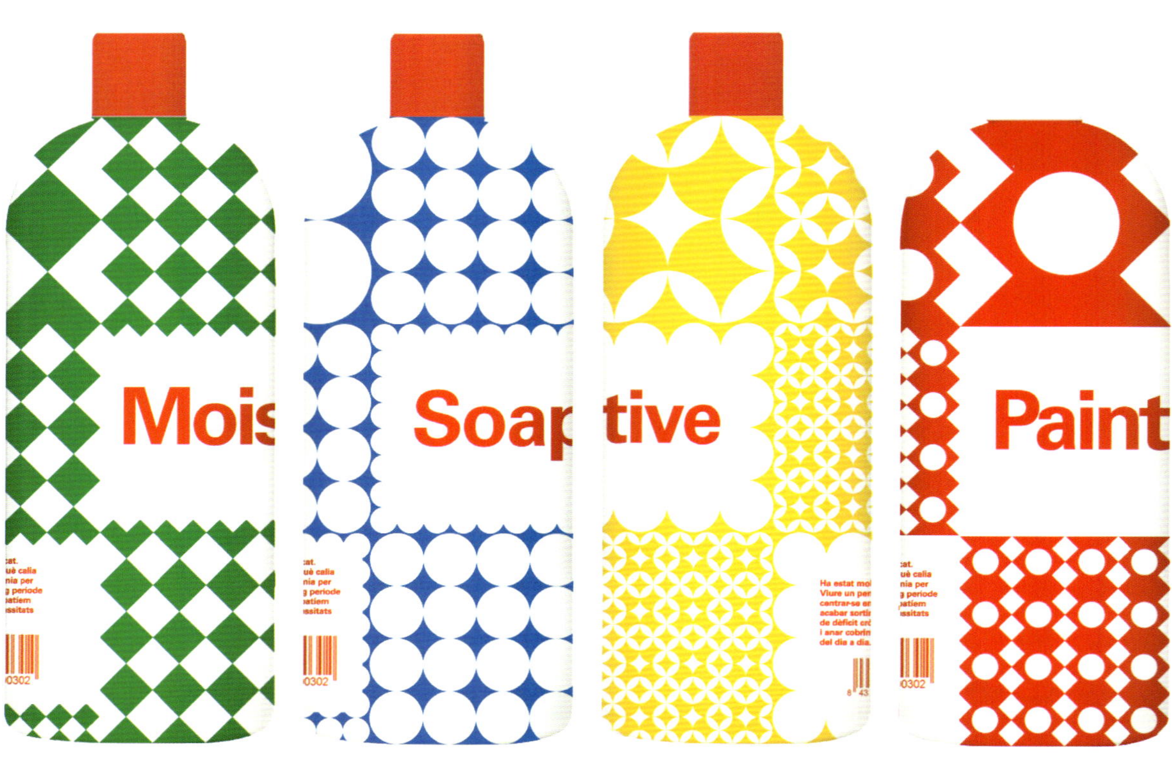

CIRCOLE, an identity created for a circus arts school, is based on concepts such as movement, fantasy, flexibility and color. The identity was built around a grid-based system to create a broad and dynamic graphic language. The logo is constantly in motion, as if it is itself a juggling game — both the colors and shapes of the logo are variables that frequently change. The system consists of 84 letters, 14 of which are combined to form the word CIRCOLE.

Design: Virginia Pol & Albert Gomez

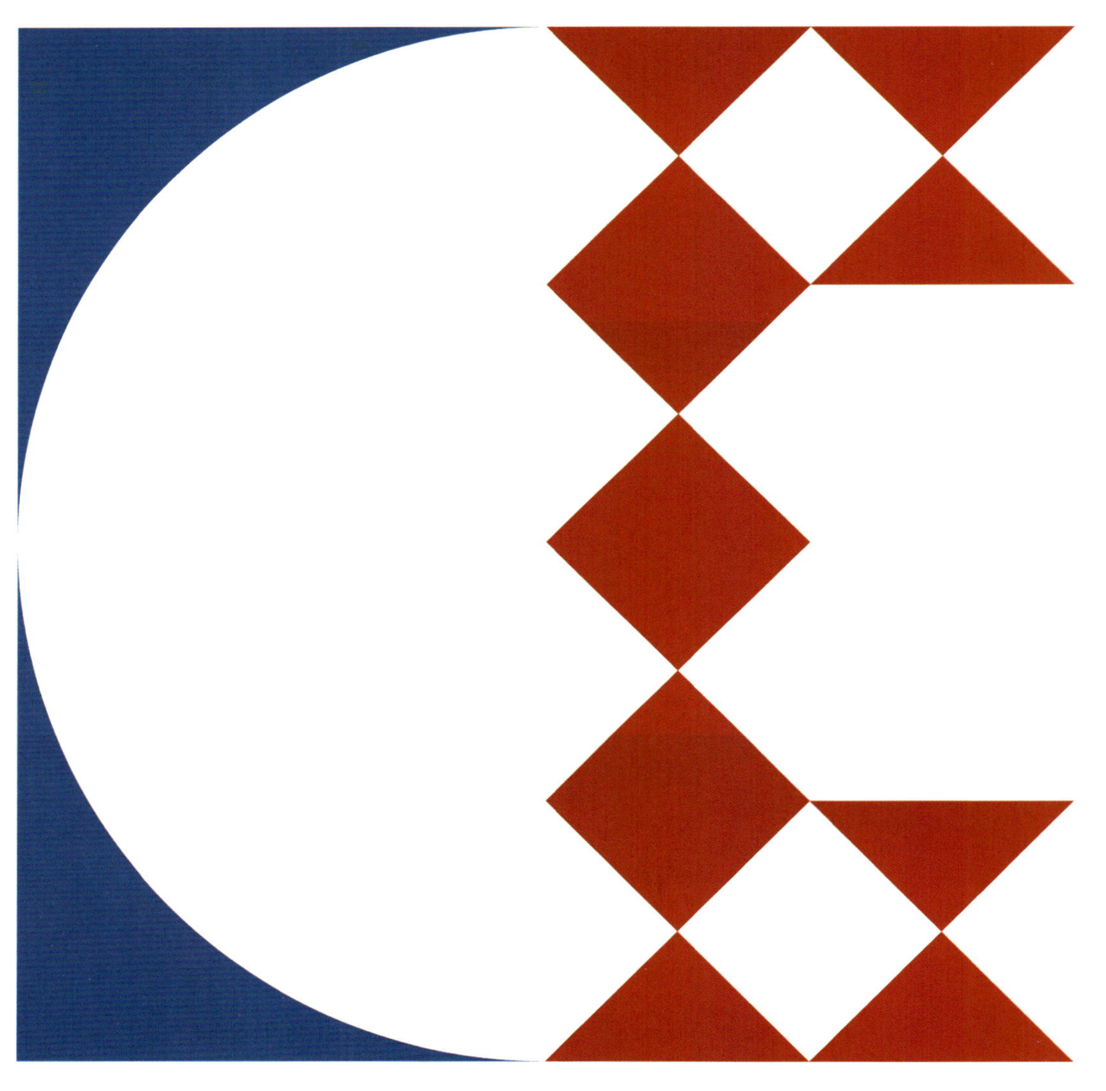

Programació
Gener — Març

Mostra d'activitats
de joves creadors

Alba Sarraute
Joan Echevarria
Albert Gómez
Quico Tur

Alba Sarraute
Joan Echevarria
Albert Gómez
Quico Tur

Alba Sarraute
Joan Echevarria
Albert Gómez
Quico Tur

Acrobàcies Aèries
de Joan Cela
i Alba Cusidor.
Charlie Rivel, Lorem ipsum
dolor sit amet, consectetur
adipiscing elit.
—
Quisque tempus faucibus
varius. Nulla ut mollis
justo.
Círcole
Escola de les
Arts del Circ
Fabra i Coats,
C. Sant Adria, 20
08030, Barcelona
933 115 897
hola@circole.com
circole.com

KixBox / Seasonal decoration. KixBox store sells street wear. Every six months they completely change the design of their seasonal decorations and marketing materials. As the main theme for seasonal decoration spring-summer 2013, Lesha Galkin chose graphic symbols of urban textures to create a kind of camouflage for the urban environment.

Design Agency: Dopludó Collective ***Design:*** Lesha Galkin ***Illustration:*** Lesha Galkin

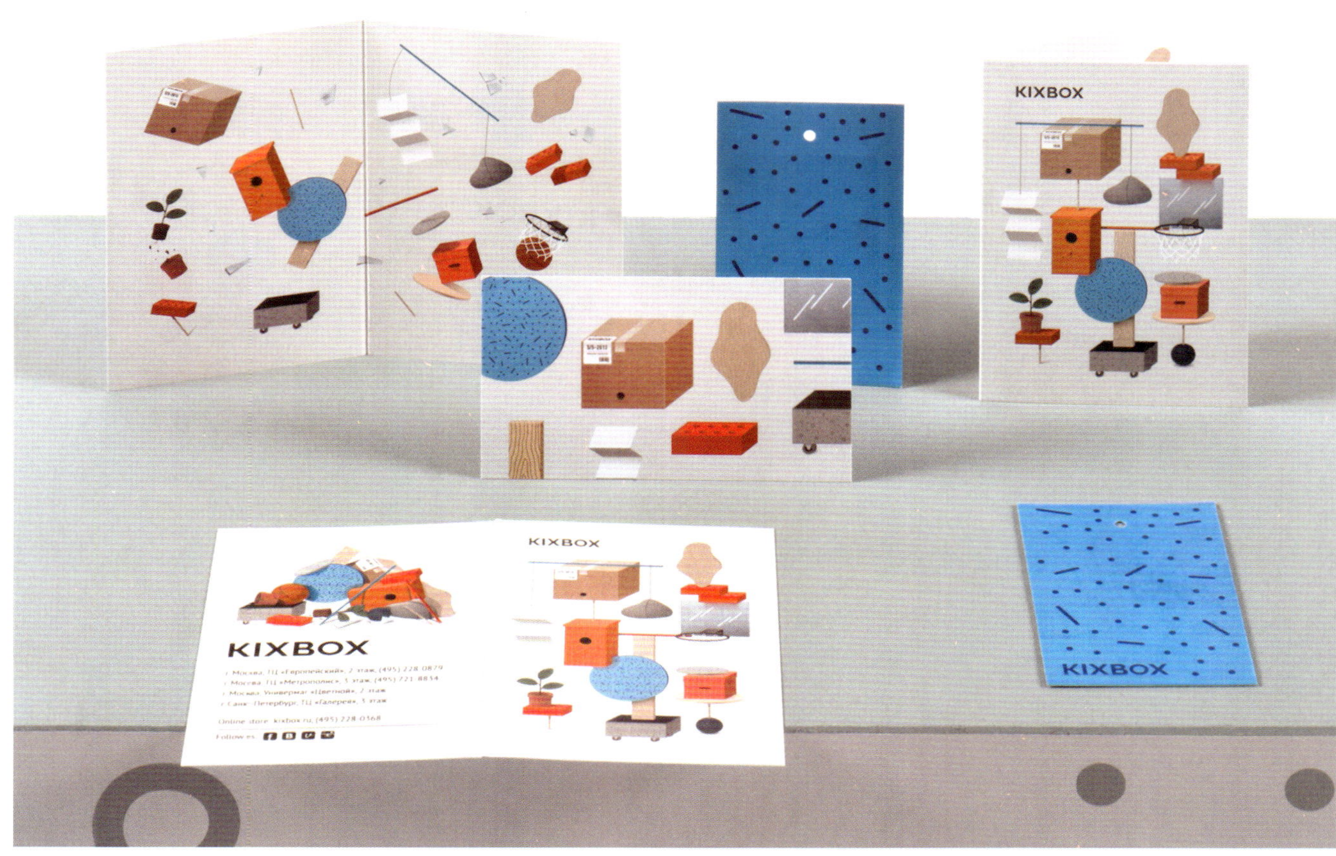
KIXBOX
KIXBOX
KIXBOX

KIXBOX
KIXBOX
KIXBOX

KIXBOX

STUSSY
STUSSY
S
A1G7
COMME des
FUCKDOWN

FORMES SIMPLES

An identity system and graphics created for the exhibition Formes Simples at the Centre Pompidou-Metz France. The identity revolved around the reinterpretation of a typeface incorporating simple geometric forms. Variations of these forms were then mixed together to create a language to represent the various facets of the exhibition, and as playful elements to denote a unique perspective for the exhibition. These forms designed to reiterate the theme of the exhibition, which draws on the senses to explore the appearance of simple shapes in art, nature, and tools throughout the twentieth century.

Design Agency: Brogen Averill Studio *Design:* Brogen Averill

FORMES
SIMPLES

AU DELÀ
DE LA
GÉOMÉTRIE

FORMES
SIMPLES

OTHER PRESS BRAND IDENTITY

Other Press is an independent publisher of print-on-demand books and multi-platform supported e-books. The logo for Other Press derives from the letters "O" and "R" that bookend the word "Other". Or is also a conjunction that signifies an alternative choice. Other Press believes that their informed customers are always making empowered choices about what they read and the format they read it in.

Design: Amrita Marino *Photography:* Greg Marino

Ibsen
or
Irving

Proust
or
Plath

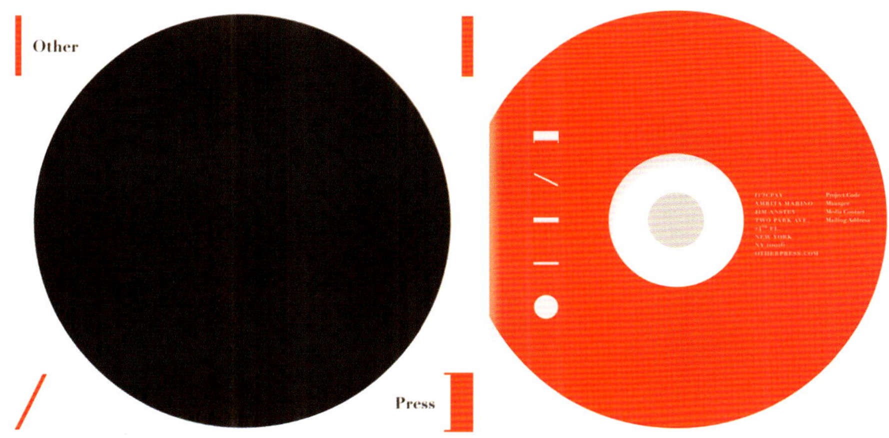

Other
Press

Other

Aristotle	or	Amis
Fitzgerald	or	Faulkner
Bronte	or	Brecht
Redon	or	Ross
Plath	or	Proust
Capote	or	Camus
Dahl	or	Dickinson
Emerson	or	Eliot
Goethe	or	Ginsburg
Homer	or	Hemingway
Irving	or	Ibsen
Jewett	or	Joyce
Kerouac	or	Kafka
Lee	or	Lawrence
Melville	or	Miller
Ginsberg	or	Gray
Orwell	or	O'Neill
Carracci	or	Calder
Angelico	or	Albers
Kelly	or	Klimt
Rushdie	or	Rand
Shaw	or	Shakespeare
Dine	or	Diebenkorn
Tolstoy	or	Thomas
Vonnegut	or	Verne
Wilde	or	Wells
Redon	or	Raphael
Gottlieb	or	Gorky
Corot	or	Constable
Beckmann	or	Bellini
Degas	or	Delacroix
Giacometti	or	van Gogh
Judd	or	Johns
Kokoschka	or	Kollwitz
Kandinsky	or	Kahlo

de Kooning	or	Koons
Tolstoy	or	Thomas
Monet	or	Miro
Tan	or	Tennyson
Balla	or	Bacon
Clemente	or	de Chirico
Socrates	or	Sartre
Wyeth	or	Walker
Ensor	or	Eakins
Basquiat	or	Bartlett
Perugino	or	Picasso
Daumier	or	Dali
Auerbach	or	Arp
Cadmus	or	Castillo
Beckmann	or	Bellini
Braque	or	Blake
Cézanne	or	Cassatt
Chardin	or	Chagall
Dürer	or	Duchamp
Escher	or	Ernst
van Eyck	or	Estes
Freud	or	Fragonard
Gauguin	or	Guston
Hockney	or	Hirst
Aristotle	or	Amis
Fitzgerald	or	Faulkner
Bronte	or	Brecht
Redon	or	Ross
Plath	or	Proust
Capote	or	Camus
Dahl	or	Dickinson
Emerson	or	Eliot
Goethe	or	Ginsburg
Homer	or	Hemingway
Irving	or	Ibsen
Jewett	or	Joyce
Kerouac	or	Kafka
Lee	or	Lawrence
Melville	or	Miller
Ginsberg	or	Gray
Orwell	or	O'Neill
Carracci	or	Calder
Angelico	or	Albers
Kelly	or	Klimt
Rushdie	or	Rand
Shaw	or	Shakespeare
Dine	or	Diebenkorn
Tolstoy	or	Thomas
Vonnegut	or	Verne
Wilde	or	Wells
Redon	or	Raphael
Gottlieb	or	Gorky
Corot	or	Constable

Press

Other

Ginsburg
or
Goethe
Ross
or
Redon
Koons
or
de Kooning
Johns
or
Judd
Thomas
or
Tolstoy
Gorky
or
Gottlieb
Miro
or
Monet

Tennyson
or
Tan
Bacon
or
Balla
Munro
or
MacLeod
Sartre
or
Sondheim
Walker
or
Wyeth
Bartlett
or
Basquiat
Picasso
or
Perugino

Dali
or
Daumier
Albers
or
Angelico
Arp
or
Auerbach
Ayckbourn
or
Adams
Castillo
or
Cadmus
Bellini
or
Beckmann
Blake
or
Braque
Cassatt
or
Cézanne
Chagall
or
Chardin
de Chirico
or
Clemente

Delacroix
or
Degas
Duchamp
or
Dürer
Eakins
or
Ensor
Ernst
or
Hirst
or
Hockney

Press /

CONTEXT: UN BAND PER GENOVA

Genova launched an international contest for the design of the city's brand. The graphic solution proposed takes inspiration from nautical flags, elements of the harbor, and the story of the maritime Republic of Genova. The word "Genova" is translated through symbolic code, defined by the connotations of the images, patterns resembling peculiar buildings of Genova, and a Mediterranean color palette. The dynamic use of the signs represents the different cultures and the many stories intertwined in Genova.

Design Agency: Solid Studio ***Creative Direction:*** Maurizio Cascio ***Design:*** Raffaele Sabella ***Copy:*** Giuseppe Marotta

lost in genova
www.lostingenova.it
lost in genova
lost in genova

lost in genova
lost in genova

RED ROOM

Red Room is the largest housing event in London. It focuses on the provision of social and affordable housing and the development of sustainable communities. The exhibition showcases the latest products and services in the housing and regeneration sector, with many dedicated features and seminars running throughout the show. Primary colors, geometric shapes, and clean layouts are the protagonists of this project, where the building world is represented with geometrical and cheerful illustrations.

Design: Clara Fernandez

Red
Room®
10 _11 June

Red
Room®
10 _11 June
Red Room®
Housing exhibition
Red Room®
Red Room®

Firefox   Archivo   Editar   Ver   Historial   Marcadores   Herramientas   Ventana   Ayuda
About   Projects   Blog   Services   Coaching
Red
Room
Housing
exhibition
10_11 June
Rotterdam
10 _Jun
Conference
Free seminars
book stand
Live Exhibition
11 _Jun
Conference
Free seminars
book stand
Live Exhibition
Red Room®

MULTINATIONAL TYPEFACE

The new team of GSK brands was created from staff from 12 different nations with experience in 49 markets, and works to service 106 countries.
To communicate their global perspective to clients and other offices, Luis Fabra created a display font full of meaning; it's based on abstracting the geometric shapes and colors found in national flags. The typeface is used for branding in new office space, and to bring color into the new office with a signage system that at all times casually conveys this unique perspective.

___

Design Agency: Grey Singapore ***Design:*** Luis Fabra

Welcome to the global and regional
GSK Hub @ Grey Singapore.

WE EXIST
TO FUEL
CREATIVITY
AS A FORCE
FOR GOOD

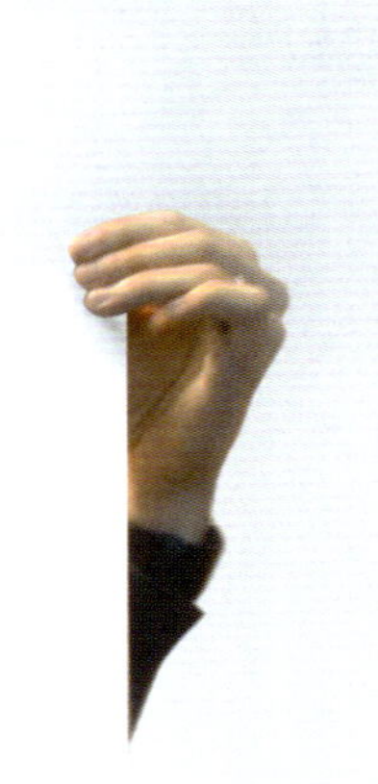

LIVE LONGER
GSK Unit @ GREY Singapore.

VOYAGE

The Voyage exhibitions were a part of the Lyon Biennial of Contemporary Art, which featured three different visions of the main theme of travel (hyper-reality, absurdity, and intimacy). The main goal was to design a strong identity that would stand out from the huge amount of events taking place during the Biennial, while staying connected with the main theme of travel. A geometric shape was created for each of the three exhibitions and used like a postcard stamp or a sticker.

Design: Mathieu Hubert

VOYAGE
ABSURDE
10
SEPT
—
2
OCT
Une exposition collective
organisée par Art-Tripping

VOYAGE
ABSURDE
10 SEPT — 2 OCT
VERNISSAGE
MAR 10 SEPT À 18H30
MICHEL LE BELHOMME
DAVID DECAMP
CAMILLE DOLLADILLE
& ITZEL PALOMO
AURÉLIE DUPIN
JULIA FABRY
KATHERINE LONGLY
CATHERINE PERRIER
1er volet de la trilogie du voyage
Absurde — Ultra-réalité — Intime
À travers le travail de 8 artistes,
Art-Tripping présente l'absurdité
d'un "voyage mental débridé,
de couches mémorielles sans
dessus-dessous", d'errances
où les paysages s'inventent.
ART-TRIPPING
Voyages d'Art.istes
www.art-tripping.com
Arc Point Trait
21 rue Ste Geneviève, 69006 Lyon
Lu — Ve : 14h à 19h / Sa : 11h à 17h
Métro B, Arrêt Gare des Brotteaux
Tramway T1, Arrêt Collège Bellecombe

VOYAGE
ULTRA-RÉALITÉ
8
OCT
—
26
OCT
Une exposition collective
organisée par Art-Tripping

VOYAGE
ULTRA-RÉALITÉ
8 OCT — 26 OCT
VERNISSAGE
MER 9 OCT À 18H30
NICOLAS BORDERIES
JULIA FABRY
MARINE LANIER
JULIEN MALABRY
LORENZO PAPACE
YVES VRANKEN
TIANTIAN XU
ZHENCHEN XU
2ème volet de la trilogie du voyage
Absurde — Ultra-réalité — Intime
Ce 2ème volet aborde les perceptions
subjectives d'une réalité crue qui
confronte nos références.
Les partis-pris des œuvres
montrées ici sont autant de regards
témoins d'un monde qui oscille
entre modernité et tradition.
ART-TRIPPING
Voyages d'Art.istes
www.art-tripping.com
Mairie du 1er
2 place Sathonay, 69001 Lyon
Lu — Ve : 14h à 19h / Sa : 10h à 12h
Métro A, Arrêt Hotel de ville - Louis Pradel

VOYAGE
INTIME
13
NOV
—
20
DÉC
Une exposition collective
organisée par Art-Tripping

VOYAGE
INTIME
13 NOV — 20 DÉC
VERNISSAGE
MER 13 NOV À 19H
ADRIENNE ARTH
ARNO BRIGNON
ARNAUD BRIHAY
SÉVERINE COQUELIN
SANDRA MATAMOROS
STEFANO MARCHIONINI
ANNE SEDEL
3ème volet de la trilogie du voyage
Absurde — Ultra-réalité — Intime
Les photographies, vidéo ou
installation présentées à
l'Épicerie Moderne mettent
le monde entre parenthèse pour
n'en garder que la substance
la plus personnelle.
Ces voyages deviennent alors
des prétextes pour partir à la
découverte de soi ou saisir
l'expérience intime de l'autre...
ART-TRIPPING
Voyages d'Art.istes
www.art-tripping.com
Épicerie Moderne
Place René Lescot, 69320 Feyzin
Ma — Ve : 10h à 17h et soirs de spectacles
Bus lignes 39 & 60, Arrêt La Bégude

Lava, commissioned by the Ministry of Foreign Affairs in The Hauge, designed a dynamic identity to ensure all events and communication during the festival year were branded in a clear and easy to recognize style.
Besides the role of providing visibility, the developed communications provided inspiration and practical tools for cooperation between the two countries in the run-up to the bilateral year by means of a movie and online tools on the website.

Design Agency: Lava **Creative Direction:** Hans Wolbers **Design:** Daan Hornstra & Ruben Pater **Web Design:** Matthew Adeney & Thijs de Boer
Client: Ministry of Foreign Affairs

Россия
Голландия
Nederland
Rusland
2013
Doe mee met het
Nederland-Ruslandjaar!
www.NLRF2013.nl

METEOPOEM

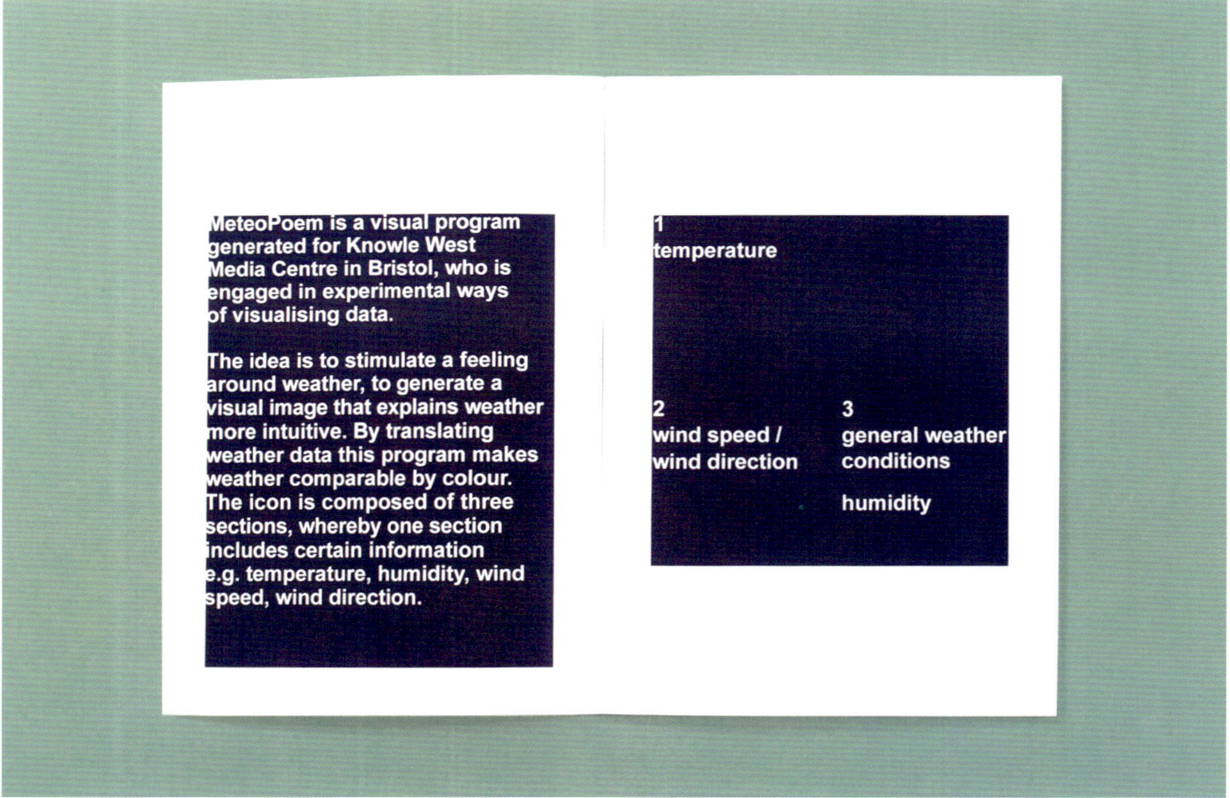

MeteoPoem is a visual program generated for Knowle West Media Centre in Bristol, which is engaged in experimental visualization of weather data. Instead of simply representing degrees with icons, Stahl R sought to generate an emotional and intuitive model of weather. By linking to live data, MeteoPoem compares global weather conditions by using color and composition. The symbols are composed of three sections, each representing temperature, humidity, and wind speed/direction.

Design Agency: Stahl R

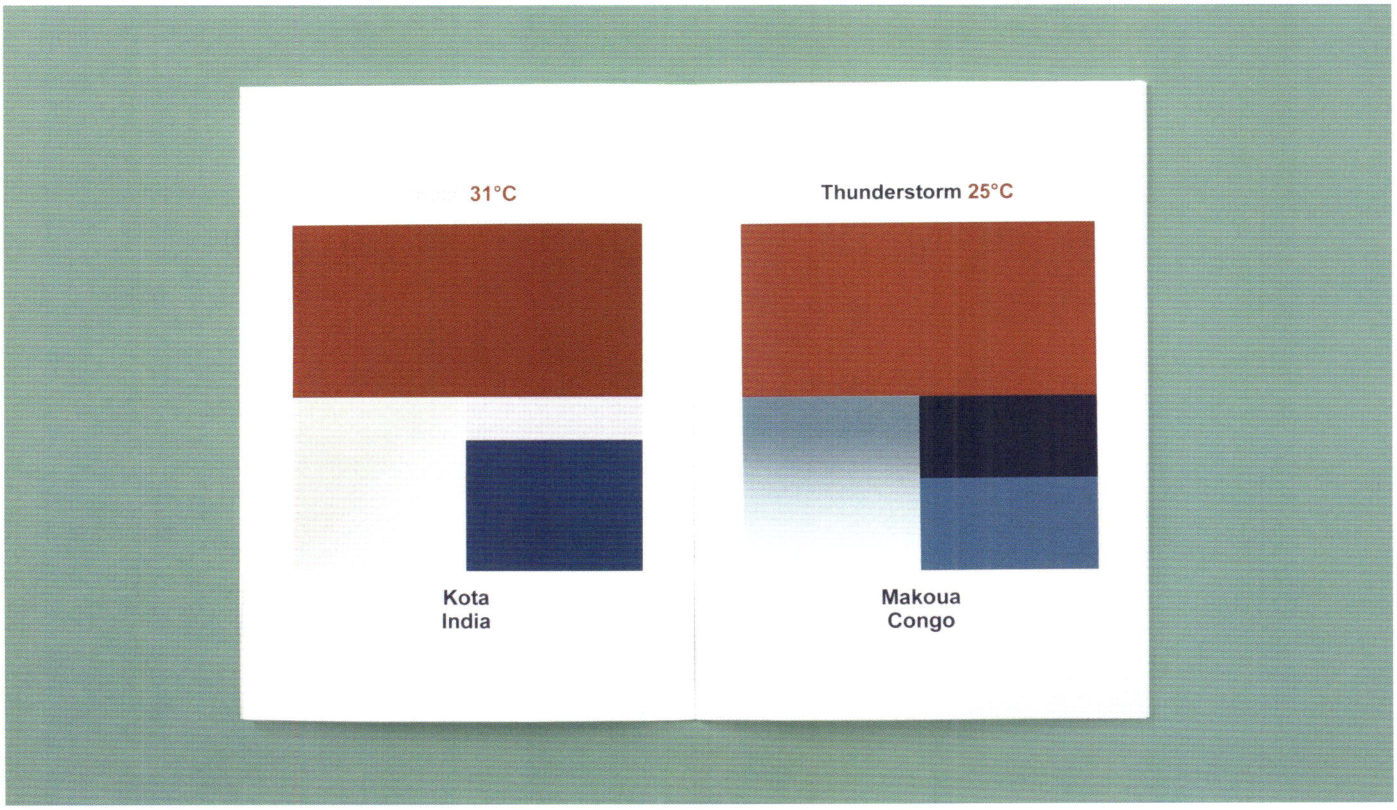

31°C
Thunderstorm 25°C
Kota
India
Makoua
Congo

RAUMWELTEN

Raumwelten, a conference that takes place once a year in Stuttgart, is a platform for outstanding works in the field of scenography. The name is a composite German word from Raum (Room/Area) and Welt (World). Here, the iconic graphic representations of each word start to interplay and interact on the flier for the 2013 event. The project was designed with and for Hort.

Design Agency: Stahl R

Raumwelten
2013

Raumwelten
2013
Die Businessplattform
für räumliche und mediale
Kommunikation
Donnerstag, 7. November 2013
Reithaus Ludwigsburg

METEOR PROJECT: A POSTER SERIES

A poster series composed for Meteor, a project about the fictional archeological expedition of a land of the same name. The project acts as a kind of encyclopedia containing graphic and textual data from the expedition.

Design Agency: My Name is Wendy *Design:* Carole Gautier & Eugénie Favre

infra-
struc-
ture
Chemin
de fer
infra-
struc-
ture
Chemin
de fer
L1
CLIMAX
Locomotive
tirant les 9
wagons trans-
portant les
marchandises
et les voya-
geurs
W1
MOTOR
Wagon
permettant
d'acheminer
des objets
volumineux
W2 LET'S GO
Wagon frigorifique permettant de transporter
des denrées et des liquides
W2
Wagon
des der
W3
EPINAL
Wagon
de colportage
(articles de
mercerie,
livres, jour-
naux, images
du monde)
(articles de
mercerie,
livres, jour-
naux, images
du monde)

Typeface Pogliotte & Typeface Wendy.

Design Agency: My Name is Wendy **Design:** Carole Gautier & Eugénie Favre

ABCDEFG 01234567
HIJKLMN 89
OPQRSTU
VWXYZ
2 WENDY
0
Typographie de titrage
VOGUEZ A MA SUITE DANS L'ESPACE SANS FIN
regular / slash / bicolor
KASIMIR MALEVITCH
LE CAPITALISME EST UNE QUANTITE DE VOULOIR NEGLIGER LA MATIERE TRAVAILLEE PAR LE GESTE
DE NEGLIGER LE GESTE TRAVAILLE PAR LA MATIERE
LE GESTE S'EFFACE
ET FAIRE D'UN SUJET SON SUJET VOILA LE PERIL DES MOTS PAR SON INTERMEDIAIRE LE PERIL DES MOTS CAR LE CAPITALISME NOUS IMPARLE
ET DESORMAIS L'OBJECTIF AVOUABLE EST D'ARRACHER L'HISTOIRE AUX MAINS DE CHAQUE ETRE
MAIS POURTANT DERRIDA ET DELEUZE L'ONT DIT LE CAPITALISME EST ANALPHABETE
MON CONFORT EST INCONFORT -ABLE
0
8
ABCDEFG HIJKLMN OPQRST UVWXYZ 01234 56789
WENDY 20 PT
OH HUM AH
VOGUEZ A MA SUITE DANS L'ESPACE SANS FIN
KASIMIR MALEVITCH
WENDY 15 PT
WENDY
WENDY 150 PT
EX1
EX2
GFEDCBA
FEDCBA
NMLKJIH
NMLKJIH
UTSRQPO
UTSRQPO
ZYXWV
ZYXWV
8765432
EX3
ABCDEFGHIJKLMN OPQRSTUVWXYZ 0123456789
WENDY 15 PT
ABCDEFGHIJKLMN OPQRSTUVWXYZ 0123456789
WENDY 20 PT
ABCDEFGHIJKLMN OPQRSTUVWXYZ 0123456789
WENDY 30 PT
ABC ABC ABC
01 01 01
WENDY/WENDY BICOLOR/WENDY SLASH 50 PT
EX4
EX5
LE CAPITALISME EST UNE QUANTITE DE VOULOIR NEGLIGER LA MATIERE TRAVAILLEE PAR LE GESTE
DE NEGLIGER LE GESTE TRAVAILLE PAR LA MATIERE
LE GESTE S'EFFACE

For this set of posters, Steven Larkin created a series of striking images that drew influence from pop art as well as Swiss design to create bold images with minimal amounts of color, shapes, and content for a simple but arresting ad campaign. Each poster references events or themes within the films being shown and depicts them in stripped-down geometric way.

Design: Steven Larkin

April 20 - May 1 2011

Box Office Hotline:
(646) 502-5296

www.tribecafilm.com

Written and directed
by: Steven Silver
Produced by: Lance
Samuels, Daniel Iron
and Adam Fredhalander

The Bang
Bang Club

TR|BECA
F|LM
FEST|VAL

Cast: Ryan Phillippe,
Taylor Kitsch, Malin
Akerman and Neels
Van Jaarsveld

SÅ DANSADE ZARATHUSTRA

Identity and poster design for Så dansade Zarathustra, a club located in Sweden.

Design: Anne Hellman Vold

SÅ
DANSADE
ZARA-
THUSTRA
FIRAR
SÅ
DANSADE
ZARA-
THUSTRA
ELIAS
ONE MAN BAND
+ SMALL FEET
21/10   LANDET   TELEFONPLAN
20-01   60 KR

An exploration in the art of reduction. This personal project purifies albums into imagery by using a strict grid that displays the relevant album details, leaving a central void to indicate the album. This void is filled by Duane's personal response to an album, which can be influenced by the cover art, a key track, or the overall flavor of the album.

Design: Duane Dalton

Bon Iver
2011

Bombay Bicycle Club
4753
I Had The Blues
But I Shook
Them Loose
2009
1:27
3:45
2:55
4:24
3:57
4:06
4:51
5:29
3:35
3:57
4:10
5:17

Vampire Weekend
4254
Vampire
Weekend
2008
Mansard Roof
Oxford Comma
A-Punk
Cape Cod Kwassa Kwassa
M79
Campus
Bryn
One (Blake's Got a New Face)
I Stand Corrected
Walcott
The Kids Don't Stand a Chance

The Thrills
4624
So Much
For The City
2003
Santa Cruz (You're Not That Far)   4:13
Big Sur   3:07
Don't Steal Our Sun   2:50
Deckchairs and Cigarettes   4:58
One Horse Town   3:15
Old Friends, New Lovers   4:01
Say It Ain't So   2:44
Hollywood Kids   5:33
Just Travelling Through   3:21
Your Love Is Like Las Vegas   2:23
'Til the Tide Creeps In   5:08

The Chemical
Brothers
6020
Push The
Button
2005
Galvanize   6:33
The Boxer   4:08
Believe   7:01
Hold Tight London   6:00
Come Inside   4:47
The Big Jump   4:43
Left Right   4:14
Close Your Eyes   6:13
Shake Break Bounce   3:44
Marvo Ging   5:28
Surface to Air   7:23

Palma Violets
4218
180
2013
Best of Friends
Step Up for the Cool Cats
All the Garden Birds
Rattlesnake Highway
Chicken Dippers
Last of the Summer Wine
Tom the Drum
Johnny Bagga' Donuts
We Found Love
Three Stars
14

Rhye
3548
Woman
2013
Open
The Fall
Last Dance
Verse
Shed Some Blood
3 Days
One of Those Summer Days
Major Minor Love
Hunger
Woman

O.Children
4366
O.Children
2010
Malo
Dead Disco Dancer
Heels
Fault Line
Smile
Ezekiel's Son
Ruins
Radio Waves
Pray The Soul Away
Don't Dig

Hurts
4802
Happiness
2010
Silver Lining
Wonderful Life
Blood, Tears & Gold
Sunday
Stay
Surrender
Evelyn
Better Than Love
Devotion
Unspoken
The Water

THE TRANSCONTINENTAL EXPRESS

The Transcontinental Express was a international arts event that took place on an abandoned train platform in the heart of Amsterdam. It explored the relationship that modern day man has developed to time, beginning with the late 19th century notion of chronological standardization, combined with the current possibilities for digital trans-time-zone connections. Inspiration was found in symbols connected to railway sign language and the notion of time travel. The choices of primary colors and classic printing techniques evoked a nostalgic tone. Twelve oversized flags, each representing different time zones, were silk screened to demarcate the exhibition space.

Design Agency: Mainstudio **Copy:** Lotte van Gelder & Clare Butcher

COLOPHON
Concept
Lotte van Gelder & Clare Butcher
Editor
Lotte van Gelder
Design
Mainstudio Amsterdam
Print
Extrapool, Nijmegen
Thanks to Museum Perron Oost for their invitation and generous assistance in the realisation of this project.
Thanks to Russer Theater Technisk for their technical assistance. And to all contributors: thank you for your time!

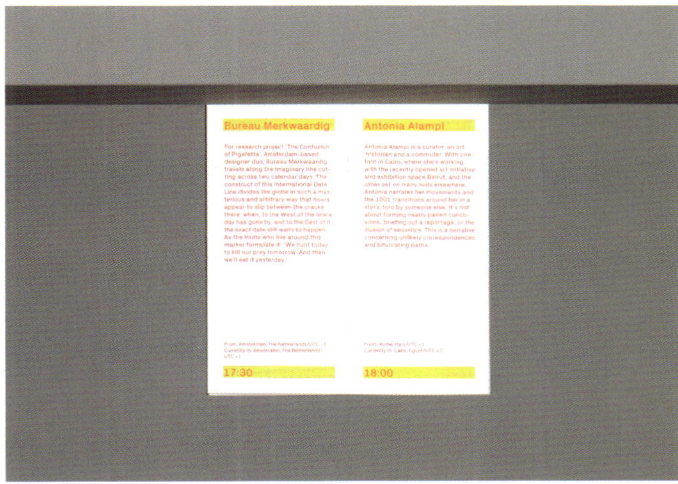

Bureau Merkwaardig
For research project 'The Confusion of Pigafetta', Amsterdam-based designer duo, Bureau Merkwaardig, travels along the imaginary line cutting across two calendar days. The construct of this International Date Line divides the globe in such a mysterious and arbitrary way that hours appear to slip between the cracks there: when, to the West of the line a day has gone by, and to the East of it, the exact date still waits to happen. As the Inuits who live around this marker formulate it: 'We hunt today to kill our prey tomorrow. And then we'll eat it yesterday.'
From: Amsterdam, The Netherlands/UTC +1
Currently in: Amsterdam, The Netherlands/ UTC +1
17:30

Antonia Alampi
Antonia Alampi is a curator, an art historian and a commuter. With one foot in Cairo, where she's working with the recently opened art initiative and exhibition space Beirut, and the other set on many soils elsewhere, Antonia narrates her movements and the 1001 transitions around her in a story, told by someone else. It's not about forming neatly paired conclusions, briefing out a reportage, or the illusion of sequence. This is a narrative concerning unlikely correspondences and bifurcating paths.
From: Rome, Italy/UTC +1
Currently in: Cairo, Egypt/UTC +2
18:00

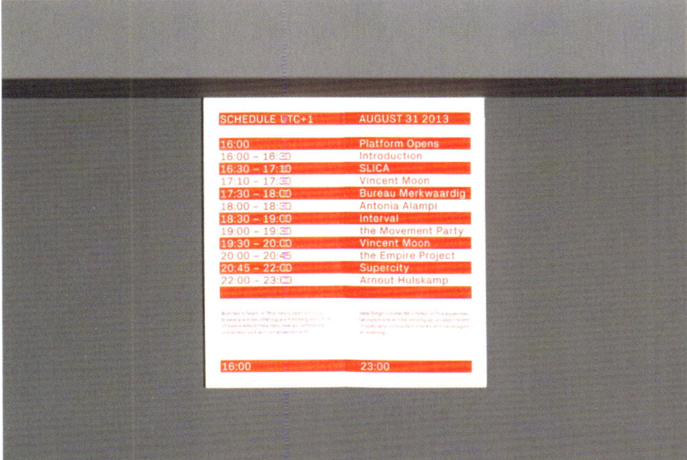

SCHEDULE UTC+1   AUGUST 31 2013
16:00   Platform Opens
16:00 – 16:30   Introduction
16:30 – 17:10   SLICA
17:10 – 17:30   Vincent Moon
17:30 – 18:00   Bureau Merkwaardig
18:00 – 18:30   Antonia Alampi
18:30 – 19:00   Interval
19:00 – 19:30   the Movement Party
19:30 – 20:00   Vincent Moon
20:00 – 20:45   the Empire Project
20:45 – 22:00   Supercity
22:00 – 23:00   Arnout Hulskamp
16:00   23:00

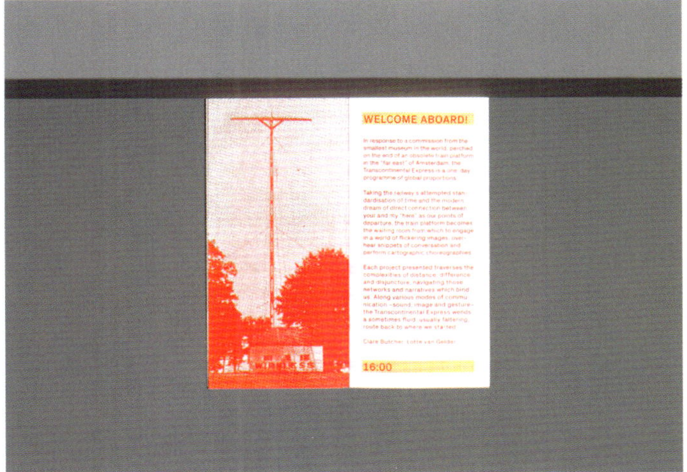

WELCOME ABOARD!
In response to a commission from the smallest museum in the world, perched on the end of an obsolete train platform in the "far east" of Amsterdam, the Transcontinental Express is a one-day programme of global proportions.
Taking the railway's attempted standardisation of time and the modern dream of direct connection between your and my "here" as our points of departure, the train platform becomes the waiting room from which to engage in a world of flickering images, overhear snippets of conversation and perform cartographic choreographies.
Each project presented traverses the complexities of distance, difference and disjuncture, navigating those networks and narratives which bind us. Along various modes of communication –sound, image and gesture– the Transcontinental Express wends a sometimes fluid, usually faltering, route back to where we started.
Clare Butcher, Lotte van Gelder
16:00

THE TRANSCONTINENTAL EXPRESS
OPERATING ONLY ON
AUGUST 31 2013
TIME: 16:00–23:00

THE TRANSCONTINENTAL EXPRESS
AM
PM
OPERATING ONLY ON
AUGUST 31 2013
TIME: 16:00–23:00

THE TRANSCONTINENTAL EXPRESS
OPERATING ONLY ON
AUGUST 31 2013
TIME: 16:00–23:00

THE TRANSCONTINENTAL EXPRESS
+1
OPERATING ONLY ON
AUGUST 31 2013
TIME: 16:00–23:00

Rocket & Wink created a new Bauhaus inspired corporate design for the "German Haus" at the 2014 SXSW Festival in Austin, Texas. The design is not only used in the brochure for "Wunderbar," but also on banners, roll-ups, fliers, menu cards, adverts, posters, and the timetable for German band performances.

Design Agency: Rocket & Wink

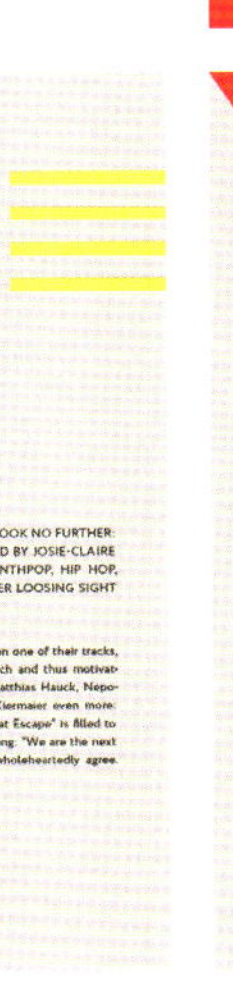
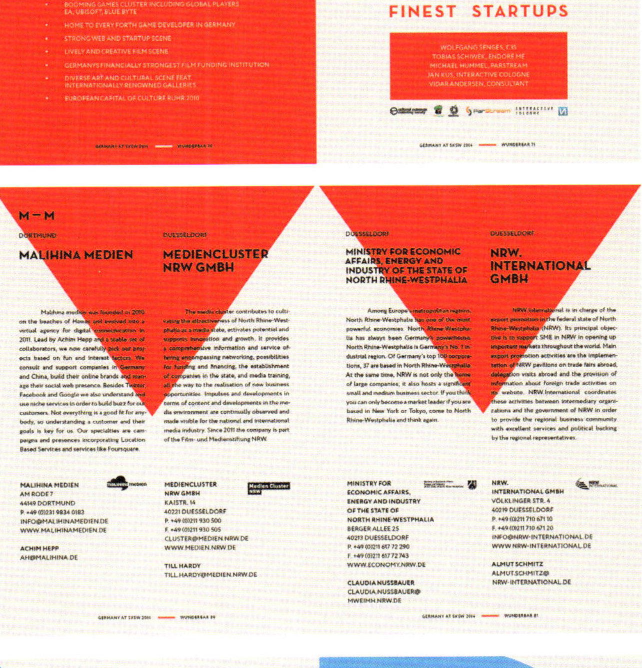

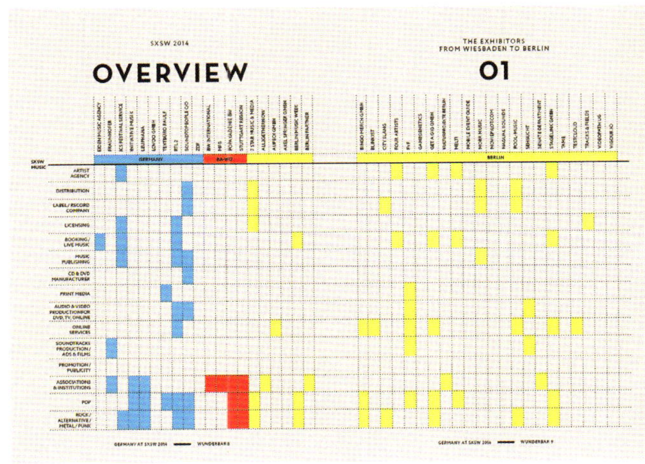
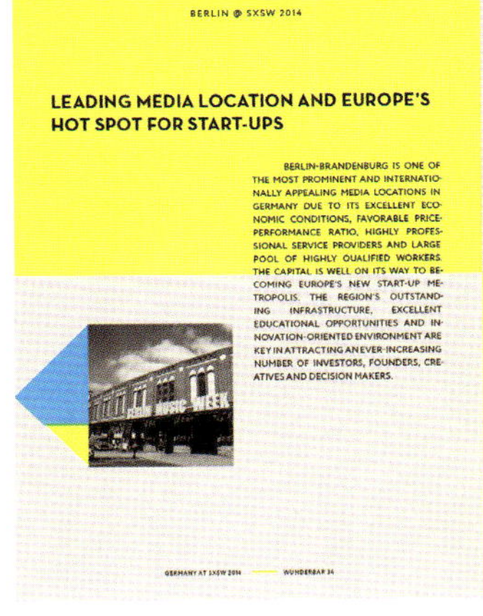
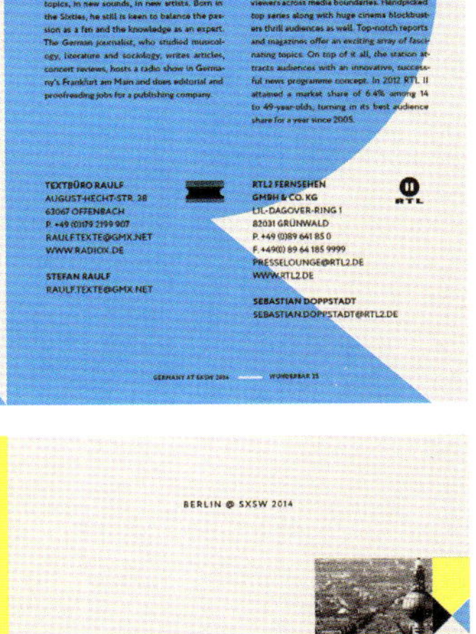

WUNDERBAR
GERMAN MUSIC AT SXSW 2014

GERMAN HAUS
SXSW
Music

WUNDERBAR
GERMAN BANDS AT SXSW 2014

A PONY NAMED OLGA
Thursday, March 13
12.00 - 12.40 am
Javelina (69 Rainey St)

Thursday, March 13
5.15 pm
Spider House (2908 Fruth St)

Friday, March 14
1.30 pm
Dog & Duck Pub (406 W 17th St)

Saturday, March 15
5.00 pm
04 Lounge (3808 S Congress Ave)

BALLET SCHOOL
Tuesday, March 11 (time tba)
Central Presbyterian Church
(200 E 8th St)

Wednesday, March 12
9.00 - 09.40 pm
Latitude 30 (512 San Jacinto Blvd)

Thursday, March 13
1.00 - 1.50 am
German Haus (77 Rainey St)

CLAIRE
Wednesday, March 12 (time tba)
Parish (214 E 6th St)

Thursday, March 13
12.40 - 1.05 pm
Empire Control Room (606 E 7th St)

Thursday, March 13 (time tba)
German Haus (77 Rainey St)

Saturday, March 15
3.00 - 3.30 pm
Lustre Pearl (97 Rainey St)

DŸSE
Wednesday, March 12
11.00 pm
German Haus (77 Rainey St)

FENSTER
Monday, March 10
10.30 - 11.15 pm
German Haus (77 Rainey St)

Saturday, March 15
12.00 - 12.40 am
Speakeasy (412 Congress Ave)

HYENAZ
Thursday, March 13
8.00 - 8.40 pm
The Iron Bear (121 W 8th St)

Friday, March 14
6.00 pm
The Romani Gallery (1900 E 12th Str)

Sunday, March 16 (time tba)
GAY BI GAY GAY

KADAVAR
Wednesday, March 12
12.05 - 12.40 pm
Red 7 (611 E 7th St)

LOUISE GOLD &
THE QUARZ ORCHESTRA
Monday, March 10
8.15 - 8.45 pm
German Haus (77 Rainey St)

Thursday, March 13
9.00 - 9.40 pm
Elephant Room (315 Congress Ave)

MONO INC.
Wednesday, March 12
08.00 - 08.40 pm
Valhalla (710 Red River St)

OKTA LOGUE
Thursday, March 13
11.00 - 11.40 pm
Lit Lounge (215 E 6th St)

MIGHTY OAKS
Tuesday, March 11
6.00 pm
Embassy Suites Austin Down
(300 S. Congress Ave)

Wednesday, March 12
1.00 - 1.30 pm
The Brew Exchange (706 W 6th Street)

Thursday, March 13
10.00 - 10.40 pm
German Haus (77 Rainey St)

Saturday, March 15
7.00 - 7.45 pm
Hyatt Regency Downtown
Austin (208 Barton Springs Road)

ROOSEVELT
Friday, March 14
11.00 - 11.40 pm
The Mohawk (912 Red River St)

TENSNAKE
Wednesday, March 12 (time tba)
Parish (214 E 6th St)

Friday, March 14 (time tba)
Hype Hotel

THE OCEAN
Thursday, March 13
12.10 - 12.50 am
Dirty Dog Bar (505 E 6th St)

WE BUTTER THE BREAD
WITH BUTTER
Tuesday, March 11
11.00 - 11.40 pm
Dirty Dog Bar (505 E 6th St)

Thursday, March 13
12.00 - 12.40 am
Metal & Lace Lounge (720 Red River St)

Federal Ministry
for Economic Affairs
and Energy

Cultural and Creative Industries
Initiative of the
Federal Government

INITIATIVE
MUSIK gGmbH

find more information at www.german-haus.biz

CIN | GOETHE INSTITUTE

A visual identity for The Cultural Innovators Networks (CIN), this project is a joint work of more than 20 Goethe-Institutes around the Mediterranean, coordinated by the Goethe-Institut Alexandria. It is a platform for communication, exchange, and learning, provided for young active civil society members from Europe and the MENA region.

Design: Salma Shamel

103

9TH ANNIVERSARY OF SALA PASTERNAK

Print design by Quim Marin for Sala Pasternak. In this visually polluted environment, which contains vast offerings for a public that is full of avid, yet often fickle consumers, Quim Marin creates fresh, memorable designs that focus on essential beauty and equilibrium to ensure effective communication.

Art Direction: Quim Marin *Design:* Quim Marin

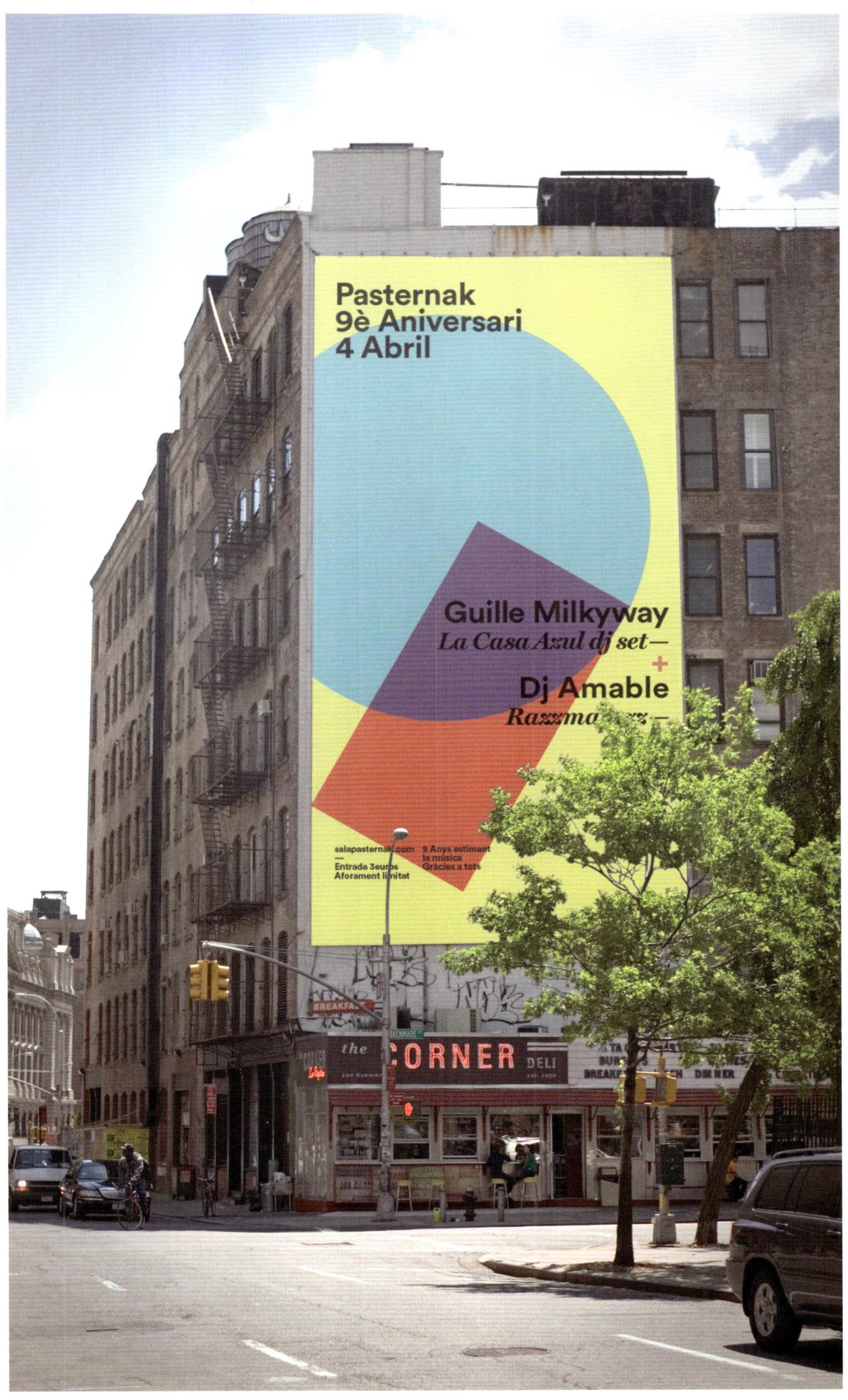

Pasternak
9è Aniversari
4 Abril
Guille Milkyway
La Casa Azul dj set—
+
Dj Amable
Razzmatazz—
salapasternak.com
—
Entrada 3euros
Aforament limitat
9 Anys estimant
la música
Gràcies a tots

CENTRE CULTUREL ITINÉRANT FRANCE / PAYS-BAS

The "Centre Culturel Itinérant France/Pays Bas" was made to promote artistic exchanges and connections between France and Holland. The mobility of this structure enables a more accurate transmission and facilitates sharing. The visual identity is centered on duotone, bitmaps, calibrated color swatches, stripes, and patterns.
Every single element refers to both national flags. The logotype is based on the shield, which represents the alliance between the two countries, merging into a single unity.

Design: Eugénie Garcia

ʃr/nl

LE CENTRE CULTUREL CONTEMPORAIN ITINERANT
NOUVELLE DESTINATION CULTURELLE
à Amsterdam du 03 au 9 octobre 2013
fr/nl

LAMBER IDENTITY

Visual identity for Lamber.

Design: Liu Yuan

ArtFad is a contemporary arts and crafts award ceremony held each year in Barcelona. Hey was commissioned to create the graphic identity for the ceremony; their end product came in the form of 500 hand-crafted invitations composed of multi-colored paper triangles arranged to form the letter "A" for the event. The final invitations were each different colors, non-serial, and totally unique.

Design Agency: Hey

MCP - EDUCACIÓN MEDIOAMBIENTAL 2013-2014

For the 2013-2014 edition of "Educación Medioambiental" materials, the client asked for one publication with three different versions of the contents. With this in mind, Roseta y Oihana decided to make a change. The final book is divided into three booklets of varying sizes (for preschool, primary, and secondary school), plus one booklet of shared content, all with the same binding. The different sizes of the booklets suggest the educational growth of the kids. The cover illustrations play with elements of the system designed to collaborate with the previous version.

Design Agency: Roseta y Oihana *Illustrations:* Oihana Herrera Erneta

En el portal educativo
www.mancoeduca.com
podrás ver la información
detallada de cada
actividad, descargar las
guías de profesorado,
vídeos, juegos
interactivos, material
de apoyo para impulsar
campañas de reciclaje,
etc. y tramitar de
forma rápida todas tus
solicitudes.

Cada centro escolar
dispone de dos claves
de acceso, una para el
equipo directivo y otra
para el profesorado.

INFANTIL   PRIMARIA   SECUNDARIA

Entra en
Mancoeduca
y realiza tu
solicitud. Cada
centro dispone
de dos claves
de acceso, una
para el equipo
directivo y
otra para el
profesorado.

PRIMARIA   SECUNDARIA

Entra en
Mancoeduca
y realiza tu
solicitud. Cada
centro dispone
de dos claves
de acceso, una
para el equipo
directivo y
otra para el
profesorado.

SECUNDARIA

LCC–SUMMER SHOW BRANDING AND DESIGN

A system that visually promotes the four main annual exhibitions at the London College of Communication (UAL). The design and branding reflected the diverse range of design disciplines featured throughout the show period, and was based on the shapes and formats of the work that could be found inside the building and around the galleries. The concept gave visitors a sense and an indication of the work as they approached the building while suggesting that there were still discoveries to be made inside.

Design: Tim Hutchinson

london college
of exhibitionists

Show 3

BA (Hons)/FdA Animation
BA (Hons)/FdA Design for
Graphic Communication
BA (Hons)/FdA Digital Media Design
BA (Hons) Graphic & Media Design

Opens from
Friday 21—Friday 28 June
Monday—Friday, 10am—5pm
Saturday 11am—4pm
Sunday closed

london college
of exhibitionists

Show 2

FdA Graphic & Spatial
Communication
BA (Hons) Book Arts & Design
BA (Hons) Creative
Advertising Strategy
BA (Hons)/FdA Games Design
BA (Hons) Graphic
Product Innovation
BA (Hons)/FdA Interior Design
BA (Hons)/FdA Media Practice
BA (Hons)/FdA Production for
Live Events & Television
BA (Hons)/FdA Surface Design

Opens from
Wednesday 12—Friday 14 June
10am—5pm

london college
of exhibitionists

London College of Communication (LCC) invites
you to celebrate the work of graduating students

Show 1

Opens from
Saturday 1—Wednesday 5 June
Monday—Wednesday, 10am—5pm
Saturday 11am—4pm,
Sunday closed

Access to HE Diploma (Design)
Access to HE Diploma
(Media Communication)
BA (Hons) Film & Television
BA (Hons) Photography
BA (Hons) Photojournalism
BA (Hons) Sound Arts & Design

Show 2

Opens from
Wednesday 12—Friday 14 June
10am—5pm

FdA Graphic & Spatial Communication
BA (Hons) Book Arts & Design
BA (Hons) Creative Advertising Strategy
BA (Hons)/FdA Games Design
BA (Hons) Graphic Product Innovation
BA (Hons)/FdA Interior Design
BA (Hons)/FdA Media Practice
BA (Hons)/FdA Production for
Live Events & Television
BA (Hons)/FdA Surface Design

Show 3

Opens from
Friday 21—Friday 28 June
Monday—Friday, 10am—5pm
Saturday 11am—4pm,
Sunday closed

BA (Hons)/FdA Animation
BA (Hons)/FdA Design for
Graphic Communication
BA (Hons)/FdA Digital Media Design
BA (Hons) Graphic & Media Design

london college
of exhibitionists

IDENTITY OF THE MUSEUM OF
CONTEMPORARY ART IN BUENOS AIRES

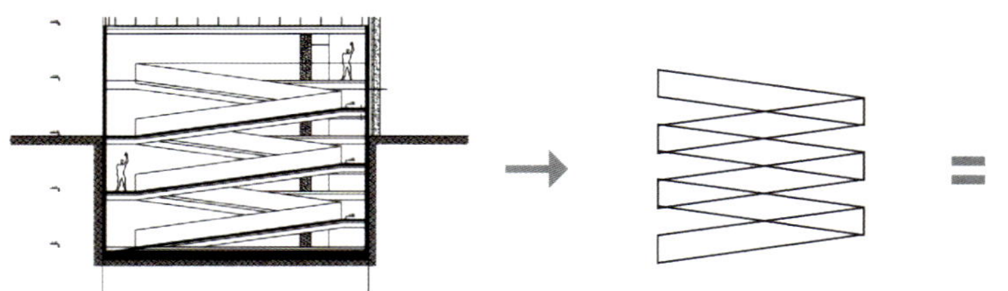

Graphic system for a non-profit proposal for the identity of the Museum of Contemporary Art in Buenos Aires, carried out under the framework of Graphic Design Degree, Faculty of Architecture, Design and Urbanism of the University of Buenos Aires.
It consists of branding, institutional archigraphia, and a graphic parts subsystem for a temporary exhibition, including signage, website, brochures, postcards, and promotional accessories.

Design: Mariana Sabattini

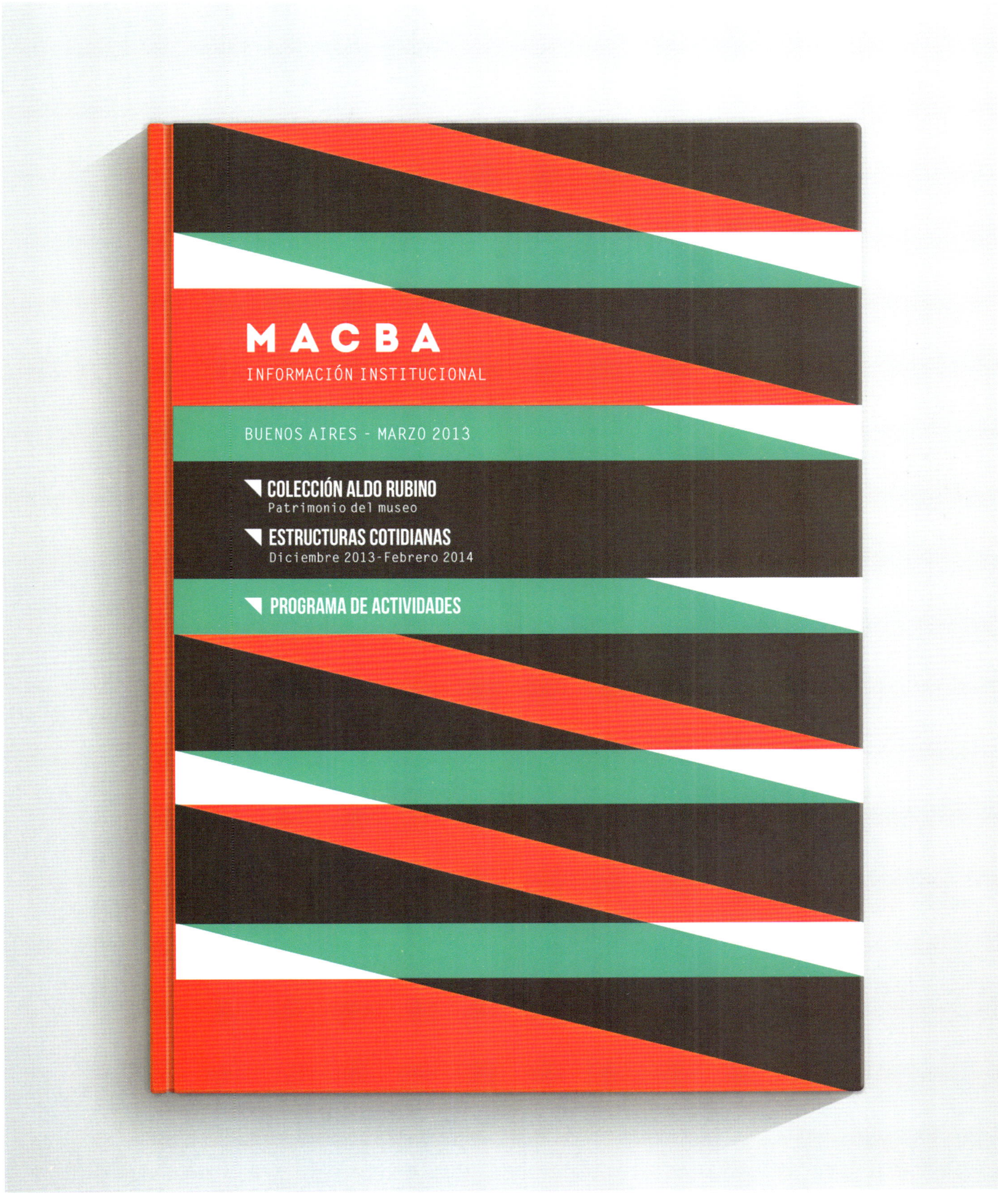

MACBA
INFORMACIÓN INSTITUCIONAL

BUENOS AIRES - MARZO 2013

COLECCIÓN ALDO RUBINO
Patrimonio del museo
ESTRUCTURAS COTIDIANAS
Diciembre 2013-Febrero 2014

PROGRAMA DE ACTIVIDADES

MACBA
CICLO DEBATES
PUNTOS
LINEAS
PLANOS
_Marina Pollonio
diciembre
06
20 HS.

SALA 01
_Pablo Siquier
SALA 02
_Valeria Calvo
CÓMO NACEN
LOS OBJETOS
TALLER
diciembre
03
17 HS.
Reservar.

EXPOSICIÓN PERMANENTE
GEO
_Artistas Argentinos
MÉ
_Artistas internacionales
TRI
Pinturas e instalaciones
CO
Colección Aldo Rubino
TODOS LOS DÍAS
DE 11 A 20 HS.

diciembre
09
19 HS.
INTENSIVO CURATORIAL
LA FORMAS
DEL AIRE
_Naomi Beckwith

FRESH TRACKS EUROPE - INNOVATION IN DANCE FOR YOUNG AUDIENCES

The identity Trapped in Suburbia created for the youth dance network Fresh Tracks Europe was transformed into their new publication, "Innovation in Dance for Young Audiences." The identity was used in six book cover variations.

Design Agency: Trapped in Suburbia *Creative Direction:* Cuby Gerards & Karin Langeveld *Design:* Cuby Gerards, Karin Langeveld, Sebastian Pataki & Richard Fussey

GENOVA CITY LOGO

Inspired by forms and colors from maritime signal flags and renowned symbols, Davide Di Gennaro & Ilaria Tomat proposed a visual identity for the city of Genova.
Each combination of symbols is headed by the one representing Saint George's cross, which helps to fix a visual reminder of Genova, while a variety of other symbols evoke a sense of the infinite variations of the city. The tagline "more to explore" reaffirms the concept of exploration represented by Saint George's cross and evokes an atmosphere of travel and discovering.

Design: Davide Di Gennaro & Ilaria Tomat

genova
more to explore
map
1   Il parco delle mura
genova
more to explore
map
2   Il porto e il parco della lantern
genova
more to explore
map
3   Architetture moderne
genova
more to explore
map
4   Funicolari e ascensor
Public transports
Museums
Sightseeing
Crafts
Gastronomy
Valid until
31 JAN 2014
Reference
AH1234567890
genova
more to explore
genova card
genova
more to explore

Nome Cognome
Mansione
Via Garibaldi 9
16124 Genova
info@genovamore.it
T +39 010 557111
F +39 010 556112
genova
more to explore
genova
more to explore
genova
more to explore
genova
more to explore
Comune di Genova
Direzione
Comunicazione
e Promozione
della Città
Via Garibaldi 9
16124 Genova
info@genovamore.it
T +39 010 557111
F +39 010 556112

HERSCHEL SUPPLY STUDIO - CATALOG & SEASONAL BRANDING

The Studio Collection lookbook design takes inspiration from the bold lettering and shapes in competitive sailing. These bold designs are used to display the race course so the boats can see the information clearly from the sea. The catalog reflects this in its large format design and pairs products with iconic racing images. The bold, oversized titles break from the usual Herschel vintage style to represent a fresh collection and imitate the yacht racing concept. This theme ran throughout all the marketing assets.

Design: Catkin Pritchard *Photography:* Stephen Wilde

DETAILS

SETTLEMENT

CANTEEN

ANCHOR

STUDIO
MARKET XL
MARKET

STUDIO
SETTLEMENT
MID
SETTLEMEN

2014 UTZON MUSIC SERIES IDENTITY

Season identity created for the Utzon Music Series at the Sydney Opera House. Named after Jørn Utzon, the visionary architect of the Sydney Opera House, The Utzon Music Series is a series of intimate chamber music performances by some of the world's finest classical musicians.

Design Agency: Garbett Design *Design:* Paul Garbett *Client:* Sydney Opera House

Utzon Music Series

Daniel Hope	Violin	9 Feb 3pm
Joanna MacGregor	Piano	6 Apr 3pm
Timo-Veikko Valve Neal Peres Da Costa	Piccolo Cello Harpsichord	1 June 3pm
Elizabeth Wallfisch Raphael Wallfisch	Violin Cello	22 Jun 3pm
Emerson String Quartet	String Quartet	29 Jun 3pm
Alisa Weilerstein	Cello	7 Jul 7pm
Bo Skovhus Simone Young	Baritone Piano	27 Jul 3pm
Nicola Benedetti	Violin	7 Sep 3pm
Xuefei Yang	Classical Guitar	28 Sep 3pm
Andreas Ottensamer	Clarinet	9 Nov 3pm

Universal Music would like to welcome you to the 2014 Utzon Music Program. We are so proud to be partnering with fantastic artists this year and look forward to this year's exciting line-up.

To thank you for your Utzon Music support, we'd like to offer you a playlist on Samsung Music Hub enabling you to listen to classical tracks for free! Head to umusic.com.au/utzonmusic to start listening.

Discover the wonderful world of classical music online with Daniel Hope, Andreas Ottensamer and more.

In 2014, look forward to:

Online Booking

We've made it so much easier to subscribe to the Utzon Music Series this year. You can book your tickets online. Just go to sydneyoperahouse.com/UtzonMusic for more information.

Subscriber Discounts

As a subscriber you save $19* on the price of single tickets. That's a saving of over 20%. All you need to do is pick 3 or more concerts to access this special price

The World's Greatest artists

The Utzon Music Series is a rare opportunity to experience world renowned ensembles and soloists in a small and intimate venue.

A Complimentary Beverage

We invite you to enjoy a complimentary beverage while you admire the stunning views and chat with friends before each concert.

Priority Access

Subscribe to the 2014 season to secure your seat before single tickets go on sale to the general public. The Utzon Room has a capacity of just 200 seats so you'll want to get in early!

Affordable Parking

The majority of the Utzon Music Series concerts commence at 3pm so you can take advantage of Wilson's Sydney Opera House Car Park $15* Sunday flat rate.

Free Ticket Exchange

We understand that plans change. Subscribers are entitled to one free ticket exchange per Utzon Music Series package. Any subsequent exchanges are $5 per exchange/per ticket.**

*Price correct at time of printing November 2013.
$15 flat rate applicable with entry and exit before 3pm.
**Fees apply, see page 27

Nicola Benedetti

with Alexei Grynyuk, piano

Sunday 7 September, 3pm
Utzon Room

MOZART Violin sonata No 21 in E minor.

PROKOFIEV Violin sonata in F minor, Op.80

ELGAR Violin sonata in E minor, Op.82

Benedetti is poetry and passion in motion

Nicola Benedetti is one of the most sought after violinists of her generation. Her ability to captivate audiences with her innate musicianship and dynamic presence, coupled with her wide appeal as a high profile advocate for classical music, has made her one of the most influential classical artists of today.

She is a violinist of 'unassuming virtuosity', and equally at home playing warhorse concertos as she is making chamber music. In this recital with her frequent collaborator Alexei Grynyuk, Benedetti gives a panoramic view of the violin sonata from Mozart's example to the heartfelt ardour of Elgar and Prokofiev's brooding and angular first sonata. Elgar's sonata in particular makes an apt showcase for Benedetti's skills. It is centred on a slow movement of surpassing loveliness – as flirtatiousness gives way to an earnest outpouring of melody sudden depths of emotion are revealed. It is a work that like Benedetti radiates warmth and joy.

From Yarmila:

If Alisa is a musician's musician, then Nicola is a people's musician. Through her dramatic and energetic performances she brings to life the sheer beauty of music, and I was swept away by her performance of Bruch at the 2012 Last Night of the Proms. No wonder this girl wins competitions! Her commitment to developing young musicians through her own program called The Benedetti Sessions only makes me love her more, and I know she will inspire many more people when she is in Sydney next year.

ORIGINE ART

This logo was designed for a new art marketing company called Origine Art, a company that focuses on sourcing contemporary and emerging art from around the world to help individuals develop, build, and start their collections. The solution marries the "O" and "A," with the "O" moving its origin within the world of art, set in an auction house "traffic light" color system across printed and digital communications.

Design Agency: Ascend Studio *Design:* Paul Croxton

ORIGINE ART©
CONTEMPORARY AND EMERGING ART FROM THE UK, EUROPE AND ASIA.
WWW.ORIGINEART.COM

BRUKEN BROCHURE FROM B TO N

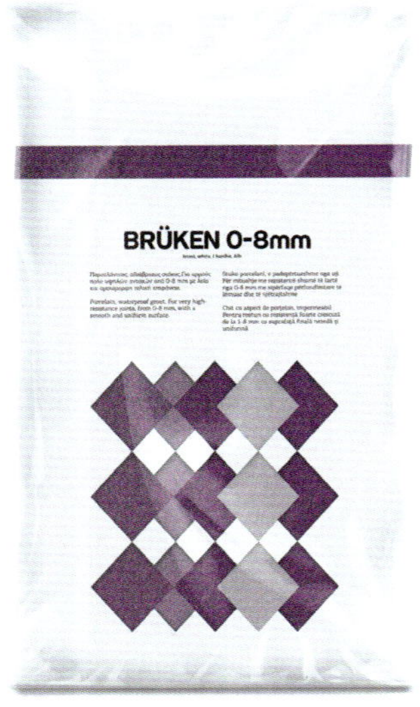
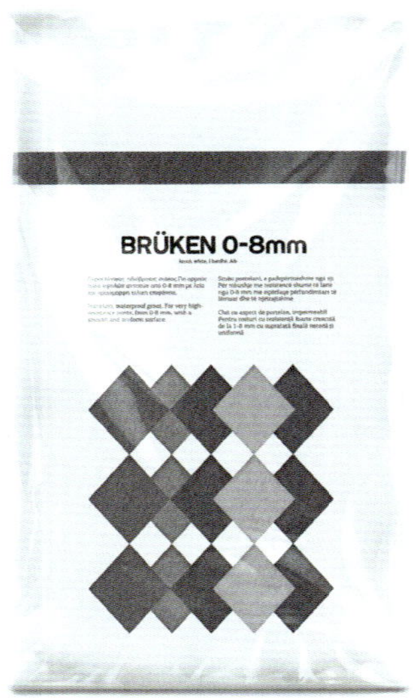
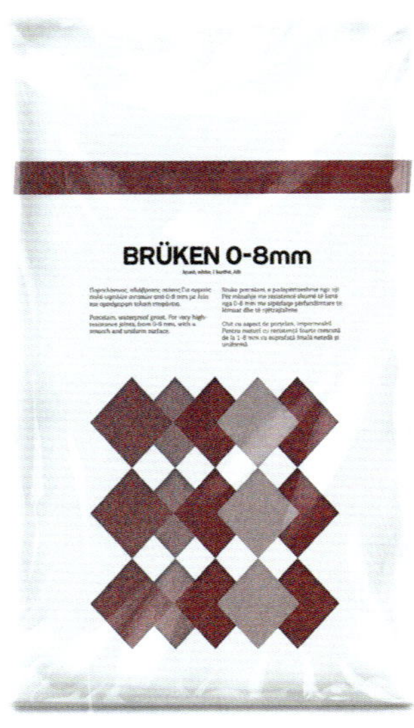

This packaging for an adhesive base, designed with construction workers in mind, uses a simple white background and an iconic tile design. Mousegraphics created an eye-catching effect evocative of stained glass or op-art with the use of diamond shapes and remarkable, bold color combinations. The final design is pleasing without being overstated, and serves as a discreet reminder of the creativity in everyone's hands.

Design Agency: Mousegraphics *Creative Direction:* Gregory Tsaknakis *Design:* Joshua Olsthoorn

BRUKET

THE FLOOR

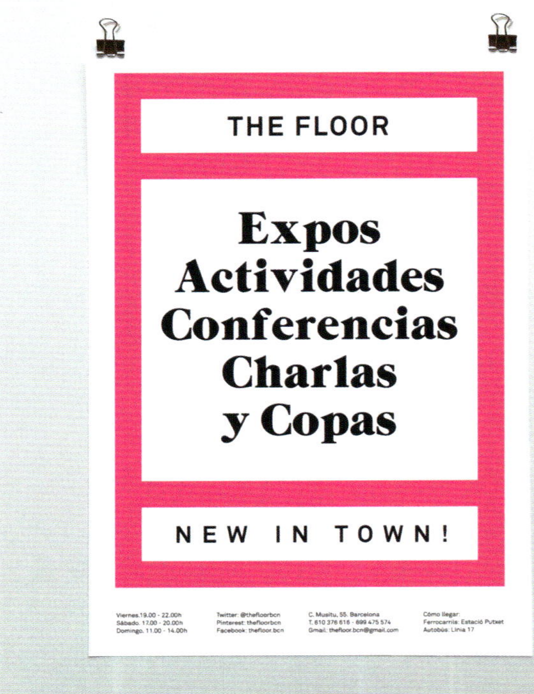

The Floor is a gallery located in Barcelona created by two partners, José Luis Bonet and Juan de Dios Pérez. For this promotional material, Roseta y Oihana replicated the facade of the gallery space, which has two large sliding doors. The two squares have a strong, unique presence that is singular enough to be paired with any typography, color, or image, while still being easily recognizable.

Design Agency: Roseta y Oihana

WORKSHOP
CARTOGRAFÍA

SÁBADO
15 DE JUNIO
11.00 H

THE FLOOR
MUSITU, 55

THE FLOOR

A R T
&
F U N

BARCELONA

THE FLOOR

ESPACIO MULTIDISCIPLINAR

JUAN DE DIOS PÉREZ
HISTORIADOR DEL ARTE
Y FOTÓGRAFO
T. 610 376 616
THEFLOOR.BCN@GMAIL.COM

TWITTER: @THEFLOORBCN
PINTEREST: THEFLOORBCN
FACEBOOK: THEFLOOR.BCN

BCN

THE FLOOR

ESPACIO MULTIDISCIPLINAR

JOSÉ LUIS BONET
ARQUITECTO
T. 699 475 574
THEFLOOR.BCN@GMAIL.COM

TWITTER: @THEFLOORBCN
PINTEREST: THEFLOORBCN
FACEBOOK: THEFLOOR.BCN

BCN

H2 REBRANDING

Identity for the art workshop "H2" (hydrogenium). The style's identity was inspired by the name of the group itself, as Aleksandra Gudymenko used specific colors and patterns chosen to indicate the gas hydrogenium. The workshop sells a variety of handmade items, ranging all the way from postcards to handmade soap. This broad variety of products was also part of the inspiration for the design's use of several different geometric patterns.

Design: Aleksandra Gudymenko

http://vk.com/h2vodorod
http://vk.com/h2vodorod
http://vk.com/h2vodorod
2
vodorod
Приморская пр. Кима

GALACTIC STRUCTURE

Cover artwork for the album "Galactic Structure" by electronic music producer and DJ Outpost. Focusing on the word structure, individual letter forms were designed using a continuous line on a grid. These letter forms were then hand carved from wood and became the 3D structures that form the album's title. With the addition of some paper cubes and pyramids, a magical scene was created that captures the ambient lo-fi nature of Outpost's music.

Design: Robert Lomas & James Hayes *Photography:* Robert Lomas & James Hayes *Photography Assistance:* Rachael Talbot

OUTPOST
GALACTIC STRUCTURE

DEGREE SHOW 2013 INVITATION PACK

Self-promotion for Jason Booth's degree show identity. He produced his own degree show invitations to send out to various companies and friends to illustrate the contents of his show. The design includes an invitation, stickers, and screen-printed business cards & posters.

Design: Jason Booth

Degree Show.

Hello! I want to invite you to my graphic
design Degree show @ the University
of Derby.

—

behance.net/jasonbooth
thisisvision.co.uk

Private view

Pencil it in!

Open
June   1   Saturday
June   -11   Tuesday   ·
2013

—

jason.booth@hotmail.co.uk
+44 (0)7974 149 039

AGENDA CCCB 2013

The Centre de Cultura Contemporània de Barcelona (CCCB) organizes exhibitions, debates, festivals, and concerts, and encourages creation using new technologies and languages.
The design by Hey for CCCB's 2013 agenda is geometric, multicolored, and directly typographic.

Design Agency: Hey

Bauhaus invokes the association of basic forms, colors, and functionalism. Designed for an enclosed performative experience within a classroom environment, the tricolored brochure (printed on a 125gsm paper) and triangular ticket stub are designed to mimic the geometric shapes of triangles, squares, and circles, primary colors of red, blue, and yellow, and the hand-held functionality that were al prominent during the Bauhaus era.

Design: Bryan Lim, Cordelia Lim, Vanessa Sim & Kyru Nisa ***Copywriting:*** Kyru Nisa

FORMEX, NORDIC CHARM

The theme of this fall's fair, Nordic Charm, salutes the blond Nordic style in combination with colorful, graphic, and playful patterns. BVD's final product was based on the construction of 3D mobiles that could be unfolded to become 2D surfaces. Each aspect of the project was done in various patterns, allowing endless combinations and possibilities and reflecting the Nordic Charm theme's aim to maximize the visitor's experience.

Design Agency: BVD *Client:* Stockholmsmässan

Meeting Point
Träffpunkten
FORMEX

AGULHA

Agulha is a textile company based in Porto specializing in tailoring and clothing. The idea behind the identity was to create a word mark that shares the same visual elements of the process of making textile themselves: a point and a line. The systematic deconstruction of the word mark served as the principle to create a playful, manageable, and systematic identity, comprised of multiple patterns and a suite of energetic illustrations that represent the independent studio culture and its individuals.

Design Agency: Epiforma ***Photography:*** Luís Espinheira

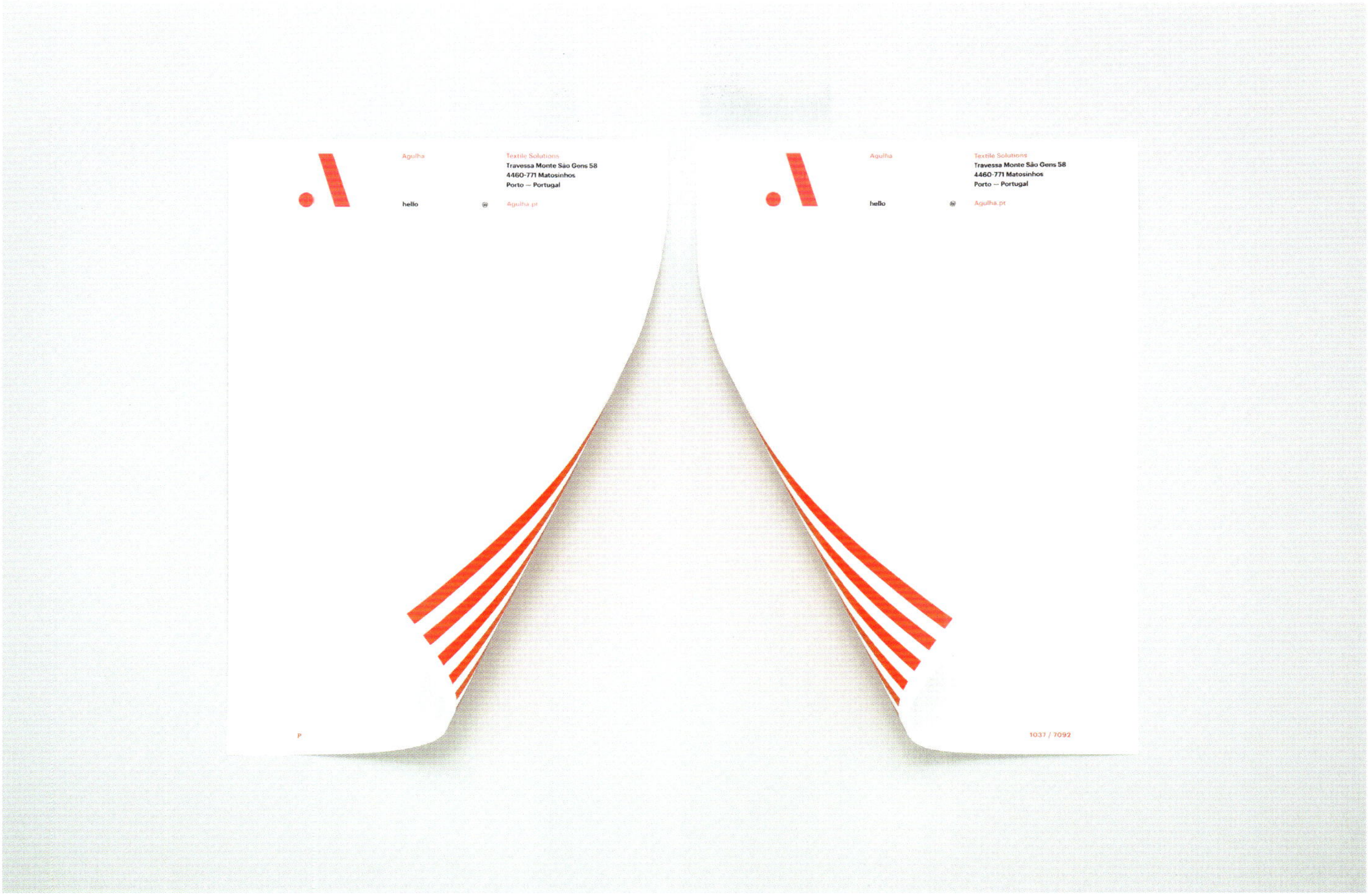

Agulha
Solutions
Fernando Valdcleiros
Travessa Monte S. Gens 58
4460-771 Matosinhos
Porto — Portugal
(+351) 91 777 23 28
Agulha pt
Fernando

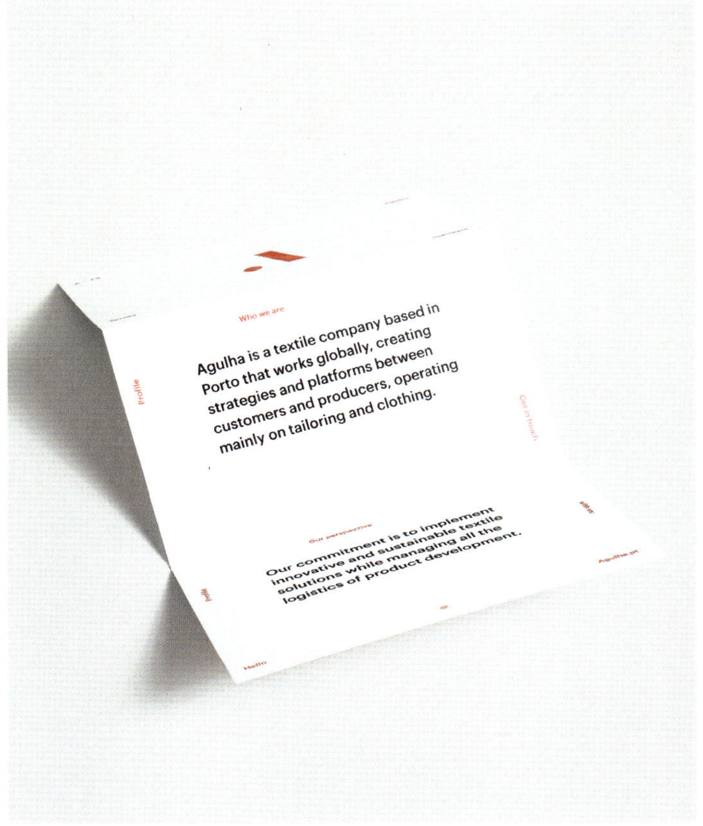

Who we are
Agulha is a textile company based in
Porto that works globally, creating
strategies and platforms between
customers and producers, operating
mainly on tailoring and clothing.
Our perspective
Our commitment is to implement
innovative and sustainable textile
solutions while managing all the
logistics of product development.

SHIFTING FRAMES

This new logo was inspired by a symbol of vintage cinema, the projector, and was designed to embody both classic and contemporary influences. It was created not only to be symbolic to various age groups but also to retain the essential essences of both film and fashion. By breaking apart the logo and experimenting with it in abstract combinations and multiple scales, the key ideas of the identity are communicated naturally to the viewer. The aim was to create a fresh and simplistic identity to represent the union of fashion and film.

Design: Kimberly Cordeiro & Marcus Lee

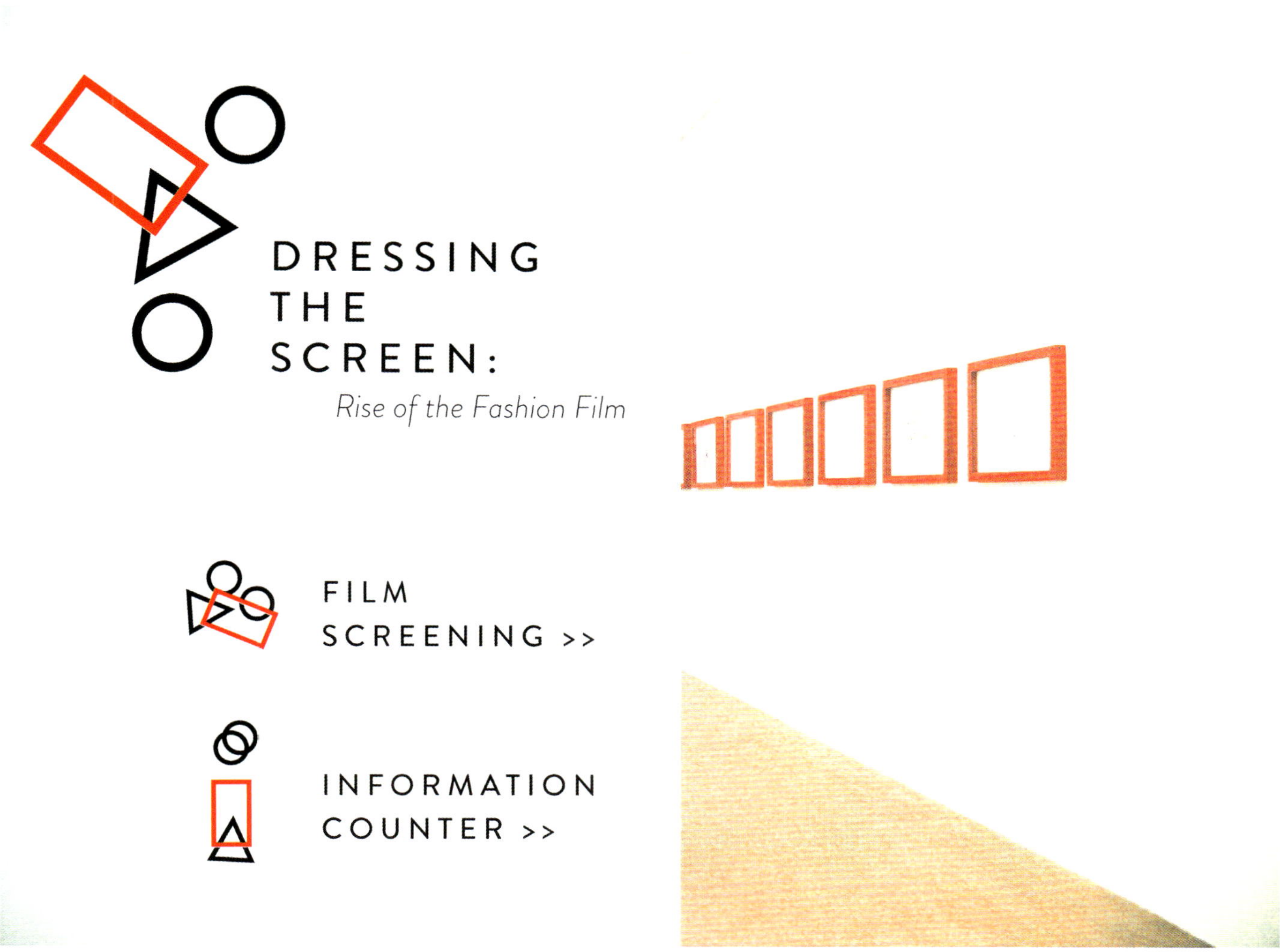

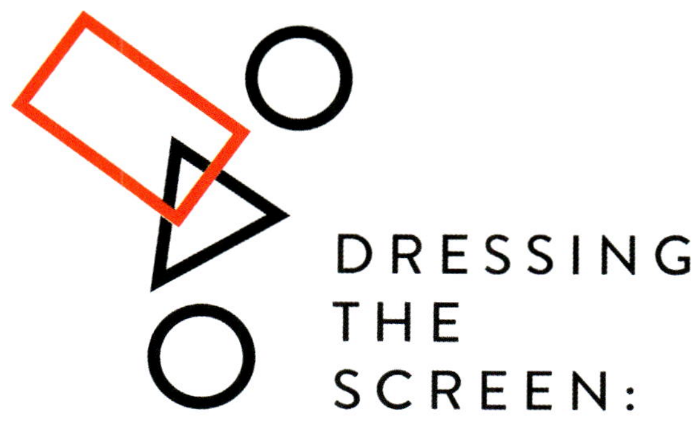

DRESSING THE SCREEN:

Rise of the Fashion Film

FILM
SCREENING >>

INFORMATION
COUNTER >>

FORMEX - ECLECTIC TOUCH

For their third time around, BVD created a design concept and graphic identity for the exhibition Formex. The project was to develop a campaign concept based on the current trend ECLECTIC TOUCH – a homage to style clashes and originality. The visual concept focused on careful touch and an affirmative attitude towards different styles, patterns, and colors in clashes and combinations - ECLECTIC TOUCH. BVD built a visual world with a delightful mix of patterns and colors in a new, brave, and original way.

Design Agency: BVD ***Client:*** Stockholmsmässan

Hey created a typographically-focused design for CCCB's opening campaign and 2012 agenda.

Design Agency: Hey

SOT BRANDING

Shapes of Things (SOT) is a new and revolutionary UK based surface and product design company for which RM&CO created a branding system based on pure geometric shapes inspired by the brand name itself. Developed to portray the "SOT" ethos and focus on a "back to the basics" theme, RM&CO utilized geometric forms and structures with playful results. RM&CO also art directed the first launch campaign, "13," to bring the Shapes of Things brand to life and will develop a preceding campaign (e.g. "12," "11") every year.

Design Agency: RM&CO *Creative Direction:* Pete Rossi *Design:* Pete Rossi *Photography:* Dai Williams *Client:* Shapes of Things

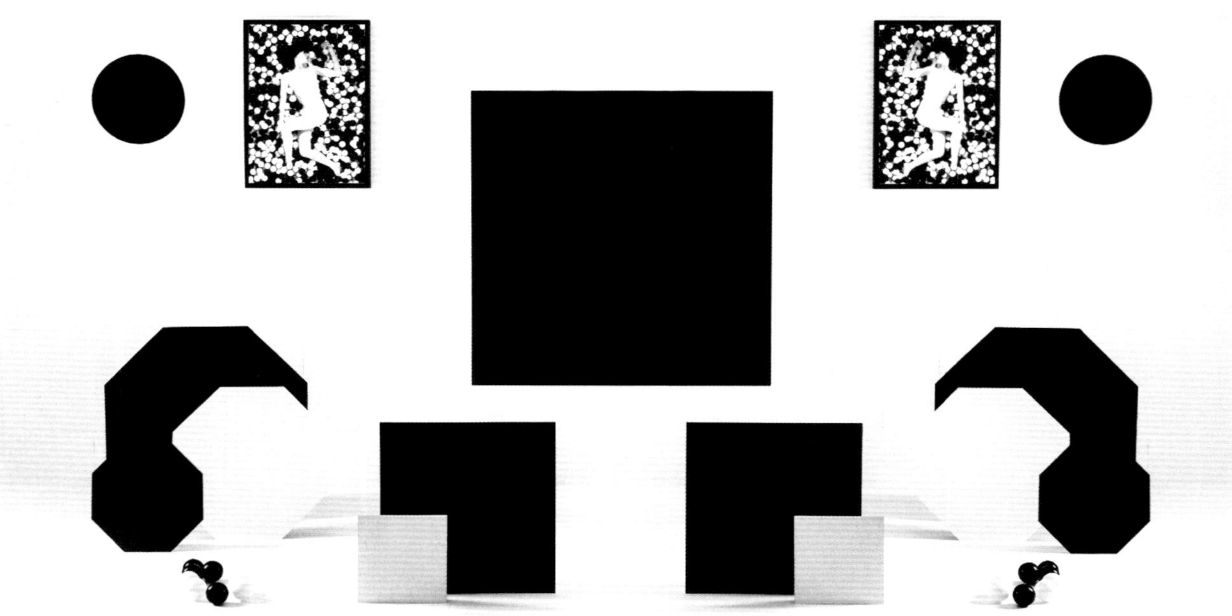

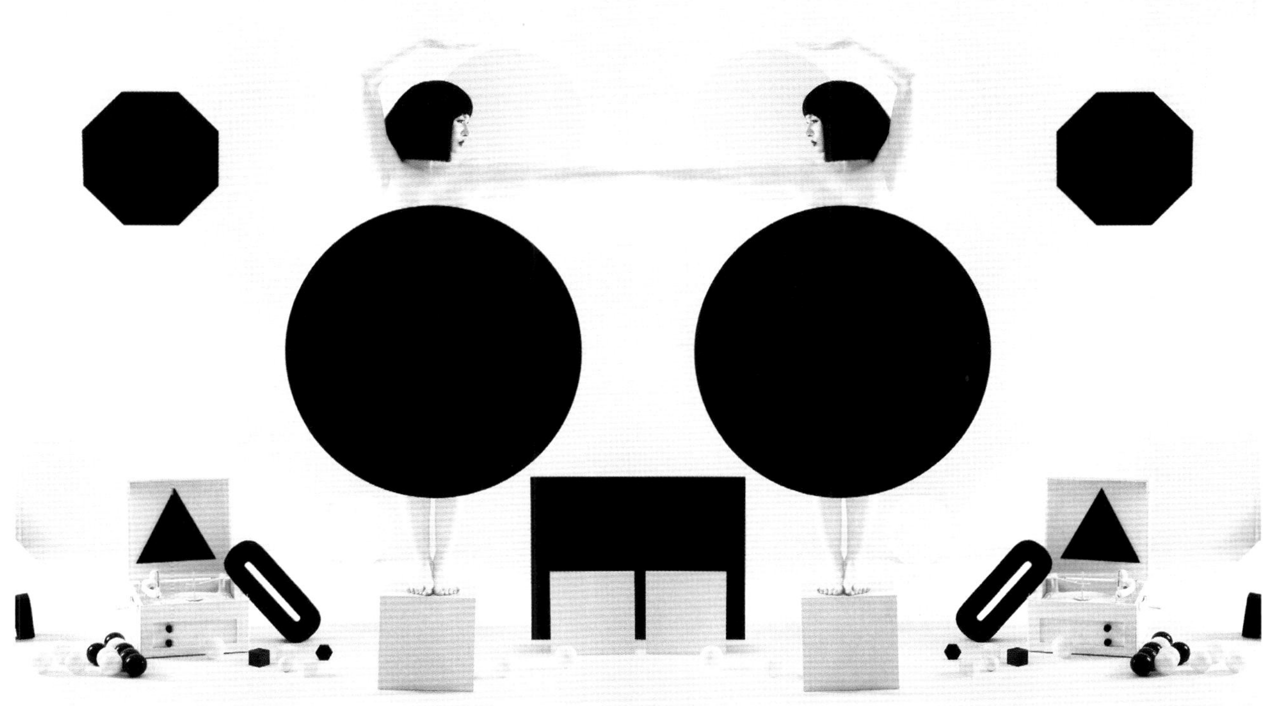

0.0 ONLINE MARKETING

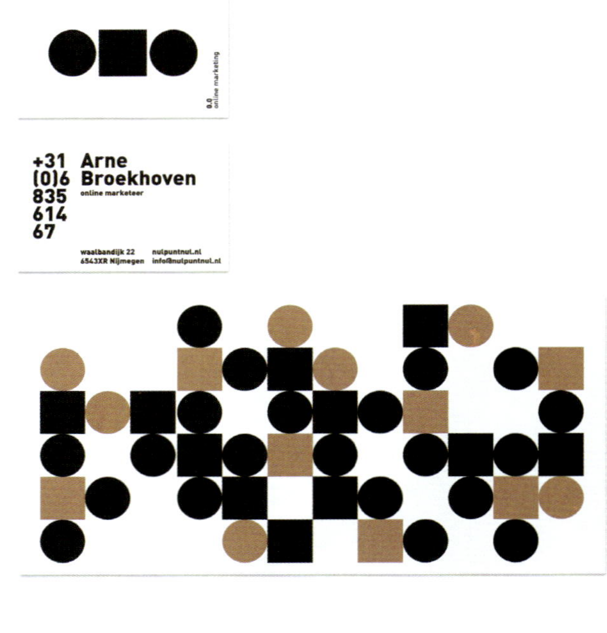

0.0 provides online marketing in its purest form, reflecting pureness and a minimalistic, clean spread of information. Studio Another Day kept that in mind when forming this project, and ultimately focused on the concepts of communication and strategy. The project was executed as a pure form of communication based on the form of a checkerboard, which revolves around strategic thinking and dynamic movement. The tan shade used was intended to reflect the client's passion for jazz music.

Design Agency: Studio Another Day

NULPUNTNUL.NL
INFO@NULPUNTNUL.NL
WAAL
BAN
DIJK
22
+31
(0)6
835
614
67

+31
(0)6
835
614
67
Arne
Broekhoven
online marketeer
waalbandijk 22
6543XR Nijmegen
nulpuntnul.nl
info@nulpuntnul.nl

0.0
nonline marketing

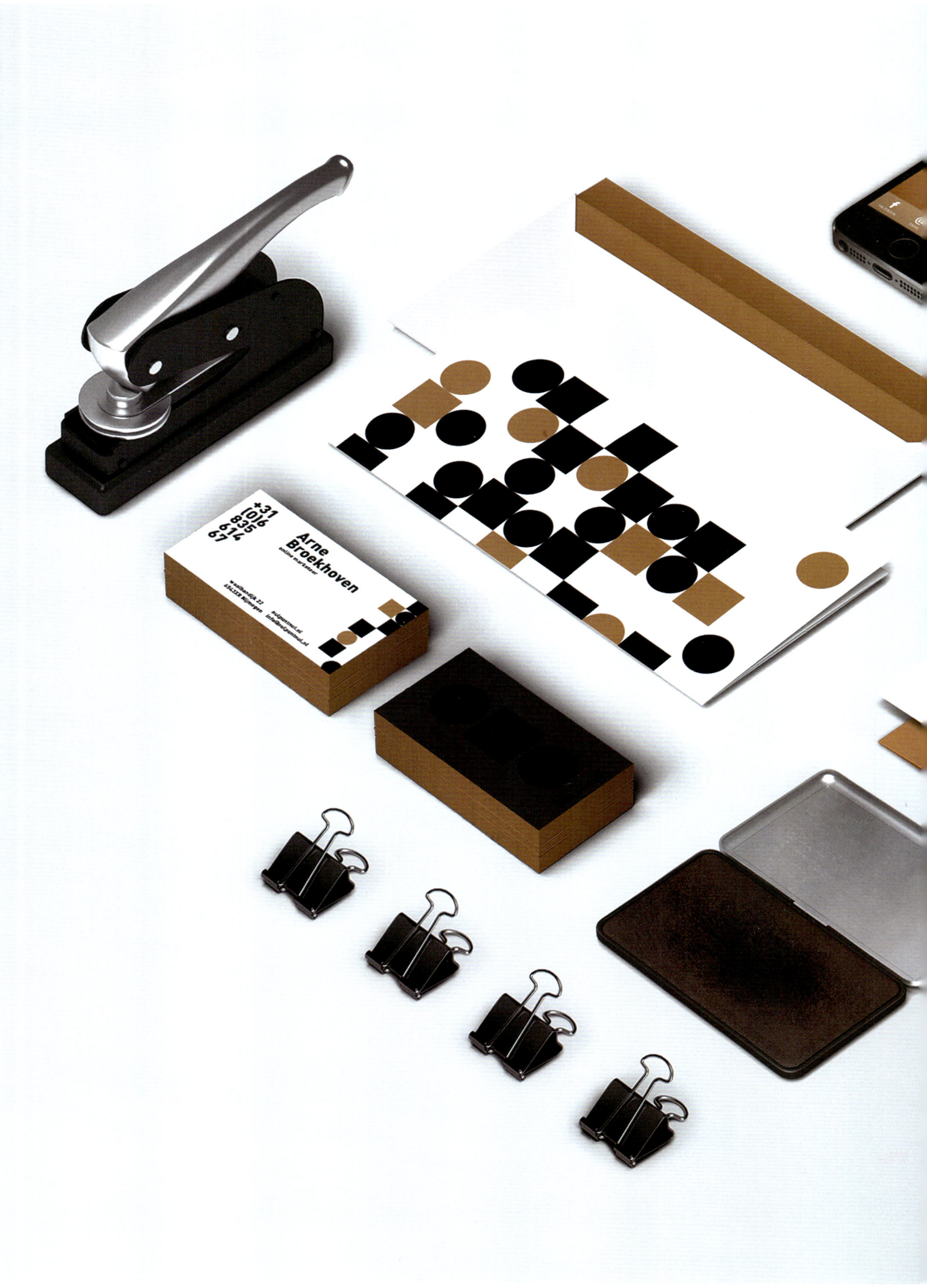

0.0
online marketing
Beste
go short,
NULPUNTNUL.NL
INFO@NULPUNTNUL.NL
WAAL
BAN
DIJK
22
+31
(0)6
835
614
67
Met vriendelijke groet,
Arne Broekhoven

LONDON BAR

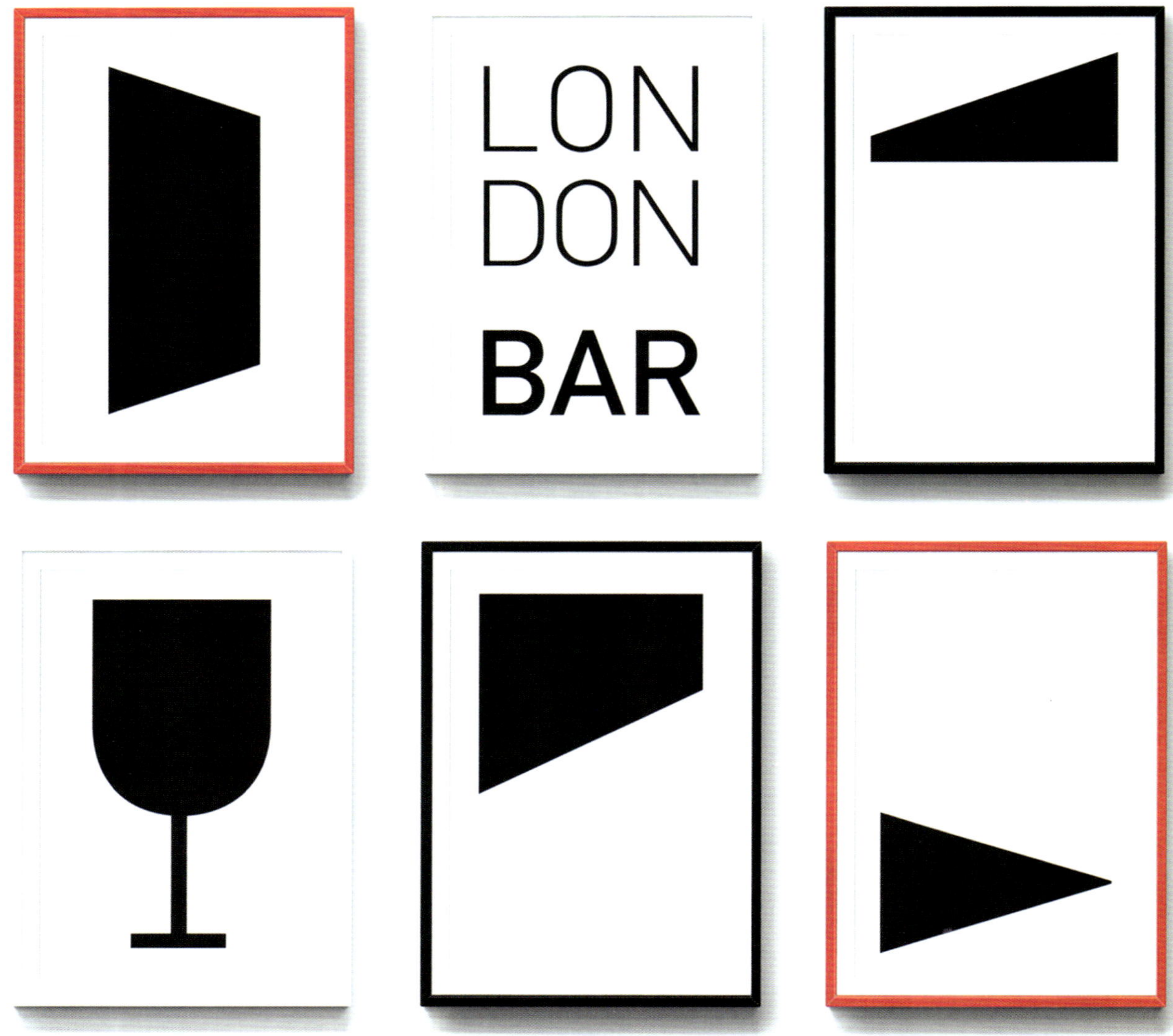

London Bar is a bar based in Greece. The focus of the identity was on clear, simplistic design, because the bar is for people who want to relax with chill-out music and a glass of wine. Aimilios Gkalipis designed a logo that would communicate this "chill" aesthetic on multiple levels while still leaving room for abstraction by rotating the word "Bar" and depicting the letters in negative space.

Art Direction: Aimilios Gkalipis ***Design:*** Aimilios Gkalipis

FRAMEWORK DESIGN ELEMENTS

Framework Design Elements was made for a small group project by Hongik University Framework (aka FRWK). It was created with the theme "Back to Basics," referring to going back to the basics of motion graphics. In accordance with this concept, the elements of the design revolve around three primary colors and a simple print of points, lines, and planes.

Design: Jiyong Ahn (Aka Anzi)

1/5
PRIMARY COLOR
FRAMEWORK DESIGN PRINCIPLES
screen based color
red
green
blue
print based color
cyan
magenta
yellow
black

TYPO-GRAPHY
FRAMEWORK DESIGN PRINCIPLES
2/5
font family
baskerville
helvetica neue
akzidenz grotesque
futura
gill sans
sabon
big caslon
typefaces
ABCDEFGHIJKLMNOPQRSTUVWXYZ
abcdefghijklmnopqrstuvwxyz
1234567890

BASIC SHAPES
FRAMEWORK DESIGN PRINCIPLES
3/5

GRID & LAYOUT
FRAMEWORK DESIGN PRINCIPLES
4/5

FRAMEWORK DESIGN PRINCIPLES
5/5
INTENTION
basic
color
typography
shapes
grid & layout
intention
BACK TO BASICS

JONNY JOHANSEN IDENTITY

The solution for designing a new identity for Jonny Johansen by Ghost was to put Jonny in a smart, conservative, clean, and delicate typeface. This was modified further to give the signature even more distinction. The negative shapes of the enclosed letters are a reference from modernism's beginnings (De Stijl and Bauhas) and a metaphor for the process the architect goes through. Other key concepts for the design were fun, openness, and basic shapes.

Design Agency: Ghost *Client:* Jonny Johansen

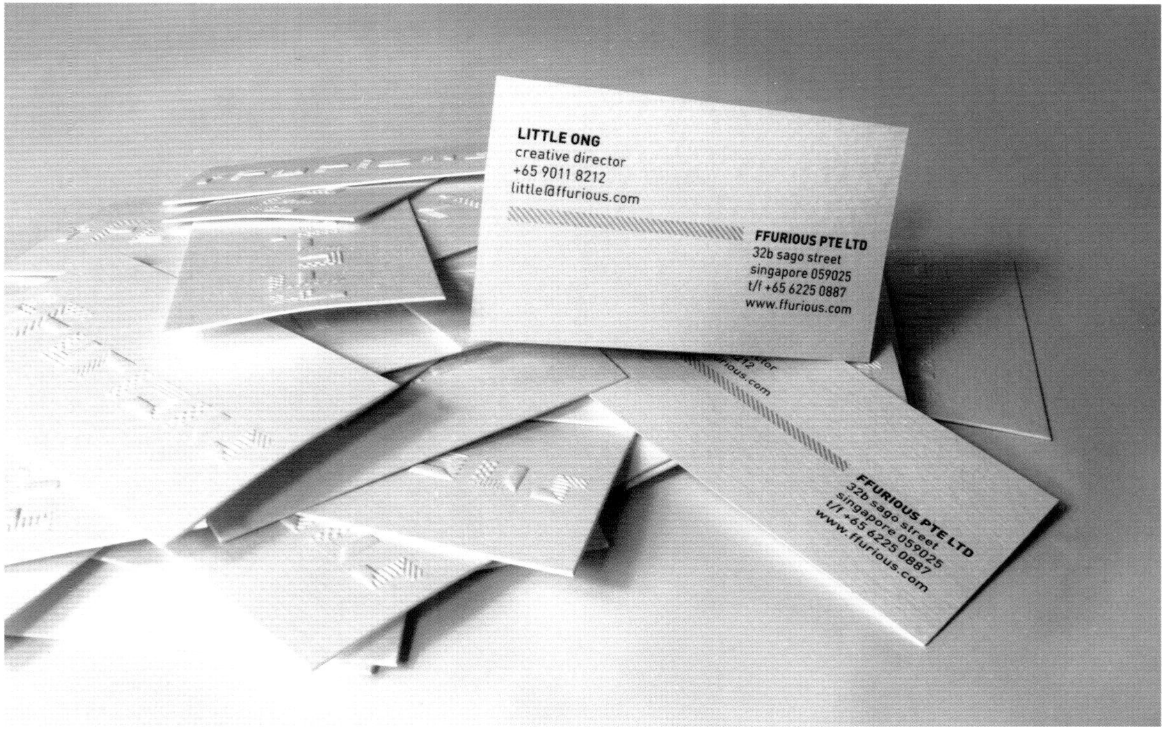

These business cards adopt a minimalist design approach that features single color printing and intricate embossing work.
Taking inspiration from fFurious's multi-disciplinary output, geometric patterns were used to suggest the various disciplines that coalesce into the dynamic form of the agency.
The geometric patterns make up the embossed mark that creates an intriguing sensory experience which delivers an immediate and lasting impact. The debossed back of the card is further sandwiched with another card to conceal the debossing.

Design Agency: fFurious

NAKATO

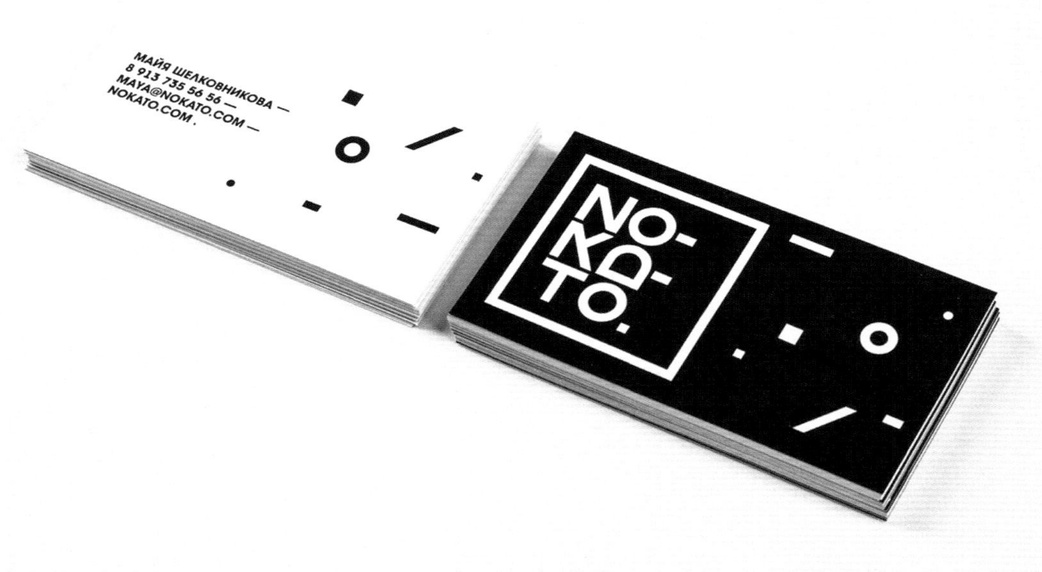

Code Studio created a photographer's logo, corporate ID, and website design. The logo is based on the photographer's nickname enclosed in a square. Geometric elements with black and white tones emphasize the streamlined style. The website easily adapts to any resolution, allowing clients to view the portfolio on any web-enabled device.

Design Agency: Code Studio

An academic project designed in ESAD (School of Art and Design, from Porto) as a branding design project for Lisbon based Roma Editorial Business. The project includes logo design, a corporate design manual, and promotional applications. The modern, dynamic logo was inspired by the simplicity of natural and organic forms.

Design: Paco Gracia Terol

CRUX

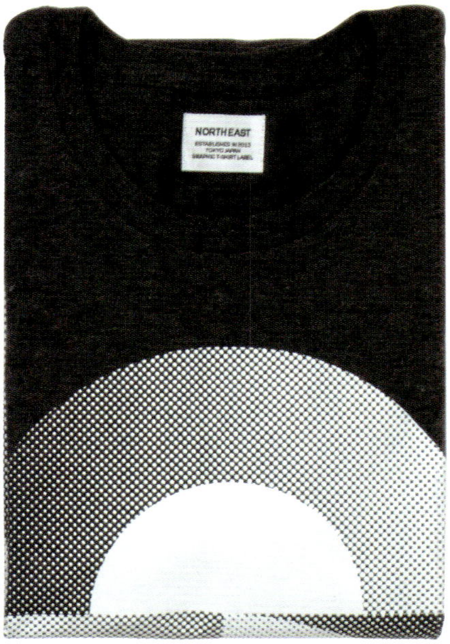

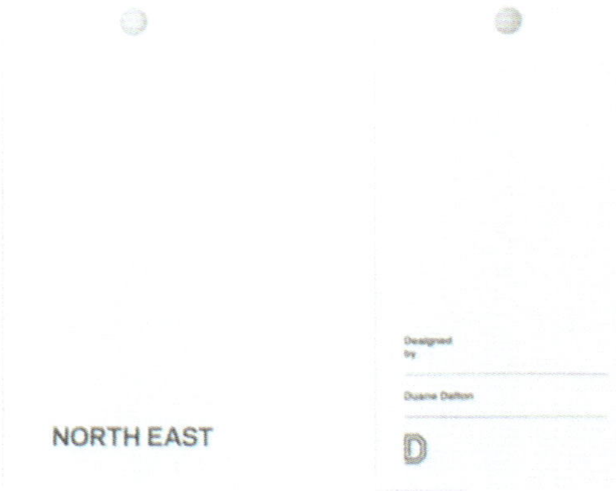

"CRUX" is a limited-edition t-shirt box set collaboration by London based designer Duane Dalton and the graphic t-shirt label North East, which is based in Japan. The box contains a t-shirt, an A4-sized print, and collaboration badges. The halftone effect was used to strike a balance between the solid form viewed when the shirt is seen from a distance and the dotted, more complex form that is apparent when viewed up-close.

Design: Duane Dalton *Production & Photography:* North East

NORTH EAST
COLLABORATION POSTER
North East ✕ Duane Dalton
Limited Edition
Black and White
210 × 297 mm
Made by North East
NORTH EAST
Established in 2013
Tokyo Japan
Graphic T-Shirt Label

GEOMETRY PASTAS

"The Geometry of Pasta" explores the multitude of pasta shapes and their history, purpose, and provenance. The book explains how to match the perfect pasta with the perfect sauce, turning an ordinary dish into an extraordinary experience.

Design Agency: Here Design ***Creative Direction:*** Caz Hildebrand

NÖRDIK IMPAKT 15

Murmure created a geometric, vibrant, and ambitious visual identity for electronic music festival Nördik Impakt. The visual display of this edition is based on a group of monochrome and geometric shapes, combined and re-imagined in textile-like patterns. The letters created from the patterns form the festival name. The project covers large surfaces on several buildings and dresses the city in the colors of the event.

Design Agency: Murmure **Art Direction:** Julien Alirol & Paul Ressencourt **Design:** Julien Alirol & Paul Ressencourt **Client:** ArtsAttack!

NÖRDIK
IMPAKT
DU 29 OCT. AU 02 NOV. 2013

NÖRDIK
IMPAKT
DU 29 OCT. AU 02 NOV. 2013
CAEN - PRESQU'ÎLE

NÖRDIK IMPAKT
AU 02 NOV. 2013
BASSE-NORMANDIE
CHRISTOPHE
WOODKID
GESAFFELSTEIN
SUB FOCUS
JACKSON
& HIS COMPUTER BAND
ARAABMUZIK
HUDSON MOHAWKE
BRODINSKI
FAUVE
BEATAUCUE
BAADMAN
JORIS DELACROIX
RONE
PACHANGA BOYS
DJ KOZE
SON OF KICK
MAISSOUILLE
FAKEAR
AUFGANG
BRNS
MAC DEMARCO
MESPARROW
GRIEFJOY
CHATEAU MARMONT
DEAD SEXY
SUPERPOZE présente «ANIMALES»
NÖRDIK AFFART · NÖRDIK INCITY
ANXIOGENE · CEDRIC DELSAUX
COURT-CIRCUIT · LEGOMAN
A.LTER S.ESSIO · Cie PARABOLE
ANNA VENTURA · RICK LE CUBE
nordik.org

NÖRDIK IMPAKT
Du 29 Oct. au 02 Nov. 2013 - Caen, Presqu'île
CHRISTOPHE - WOODKID - GESAFFELSTEIN Live - SUB FOCUS Live
JACKSON & HIS COMPUTER BAND - ARAABMUZIK - HUDSON MOHAWKE
BRODINSKI - FAUVE - BEATAUCUE - BAADMAN - JORIS DELACROIX
RONE Live (Tohu Bohu Tour) - MAISSOUILLE - FAKEAR - AUFGANG
BRNS - DEAD SEXY - MAC DEMARCO - PACHANGA BOYS - DJ KOZE
MESPARROW - SON OF KICK - GRIEFJOY - CHATEAU MARMONT
SUPERPOZE présente «ANIMALES» - CEDRIC DELSAUX «Dark Lens» ...

BERGEN INTERNATIONAL FESTIVAL

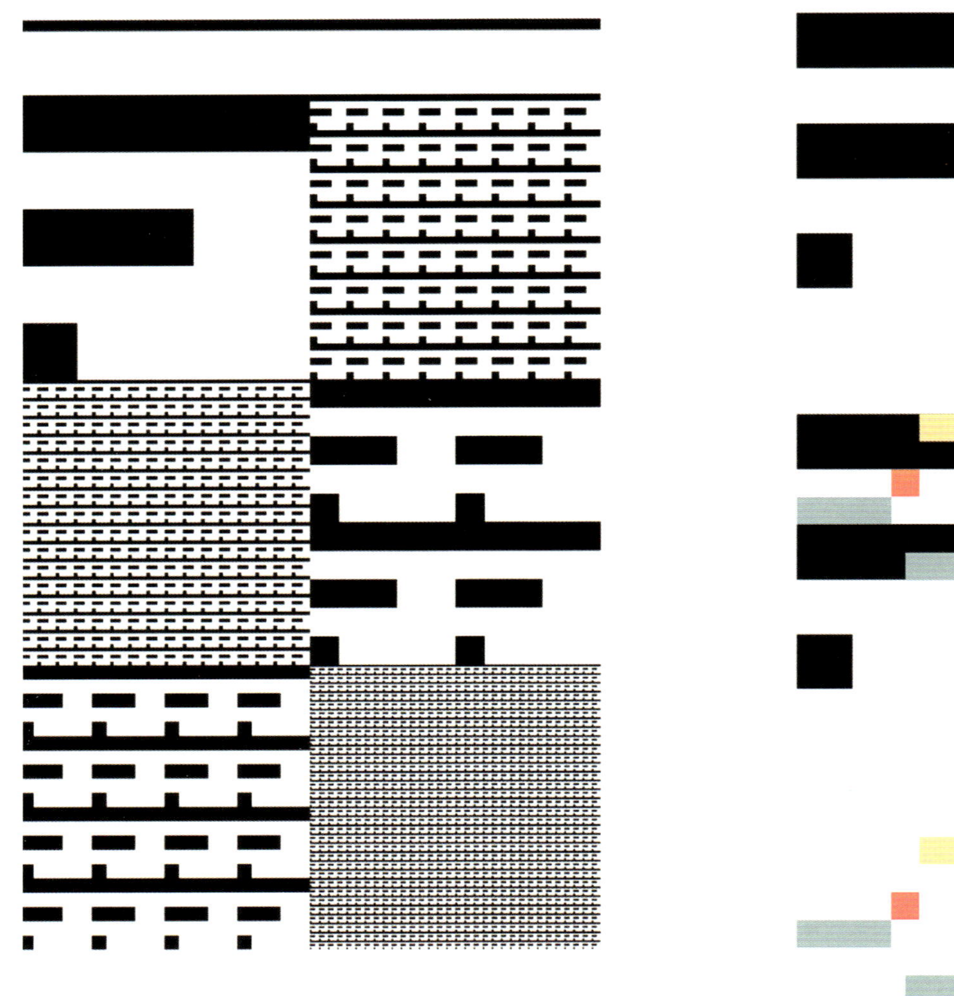

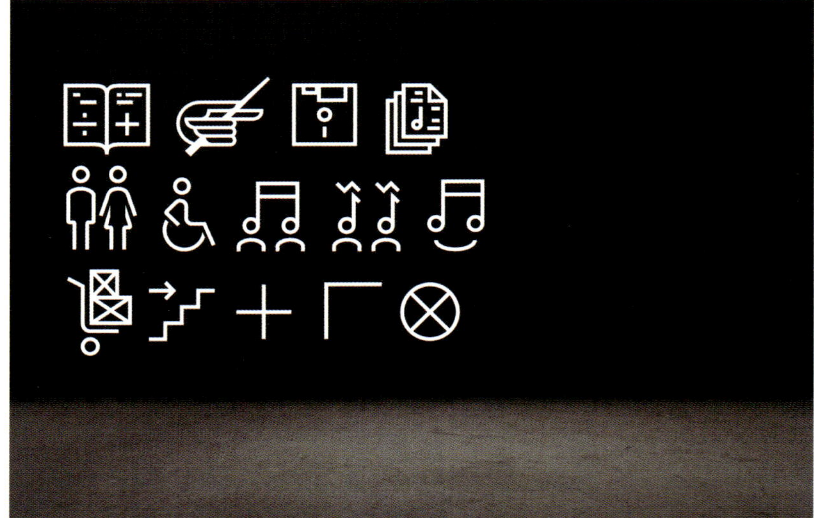

FOR ONE AND ALL. With content spanning from accessible street performances through traditional classical symphonies to the avant-garde, Anti created a visual language that could speak for them all while still speaking in one unified voice.

Design Agency: Anti *Creative Direction:* Endre Berentzen, Eric Amaral Rohter & Robert Dalen *Design:* Sindre Holm, Fredrik Eive Refsli & Elijah A. Chote
Photography: Fred Jonny™

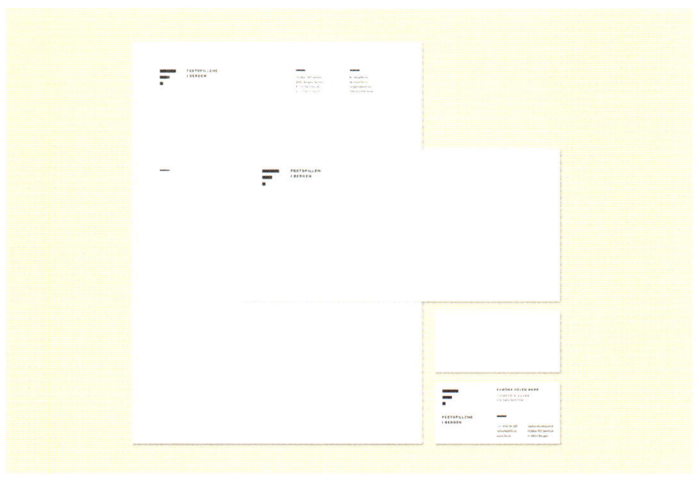

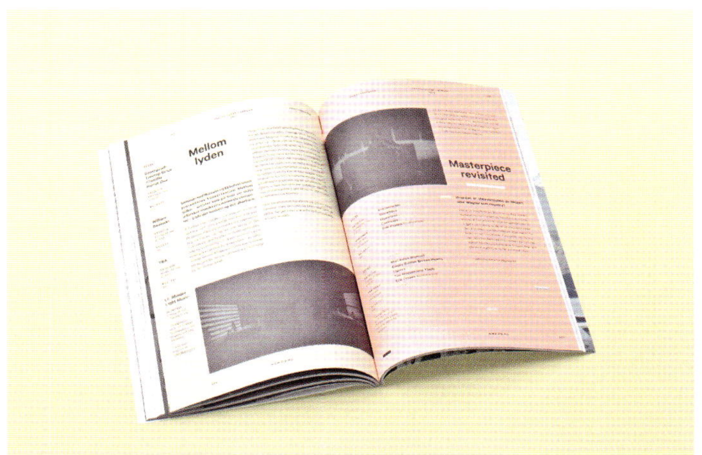

Program & billetter

Se hele festspillprogrammet på www.fib.no
www.billettservice.no /
tlf. 815 33 133

22. mai — 5. juni 2013

Festspillene i Bergen
byr på 15 dager med musikk
og scenekunst

FESTSPILLENE
I BERGEN

GRIEGHALLEN
29. MAI

SE MER
WWW.FIB.NO

Efterklang
/m/KORK

DRØMMEPOP
MED FULLT
ORKESTER

SAMARBEIDSPARTNERE FOR FESTSPILLENE

DNB

Statoil

Bergens Tidende

Radisson BLU
HOTEL NORGE, BERGEN

DagensNæringsliv

FESTSPILLENE
I BERGEN

FASHION WALK FASHION DESTINATION

Fashion Walk is a popular outdoor shopping area in Hong Kong. Blow developed the key visuals with different collaterals and environmental graphic designs for their Fashion Walk Fashion Destination campaign to showcase the multitude of fashion and lifestyle brands that can be found in Fashion Walk.

Design Agency: Blow *Design:* Ken Lo

FASHION
WALK
FASHION
DESTINATION
FASHION WALK 名店坊

AOO is a new store and brand in Barcelona. The graphic design reflects the brand's trilingual character. The names of the product are displayed on three sides, arranged on a line that serves to frame the different formats. Typography and other dynamic elements are positioned along this line according to a 3x3x3 grid. The identity is completed with three different color shades that range from light to dark according to their function.

Design Agency: Raw Color

AOO

TAMBORET
TABURETE
STOOL **TRIPO**

OTHERTHINGS

FET PER
HECHO POR
MADE BY **AOO**

ALTRESCOSES

DISSENYAT PER
DISEÑADO POR
DESIGNED BY **MARC MORRO**

OTRASCOSAS

Sèneca 8
Barcelona 08006

info@altrescoses.cat
+34 93 250 82 54

www.altrescoses.cat
www.otrascosas.es
www.otherthings.eu

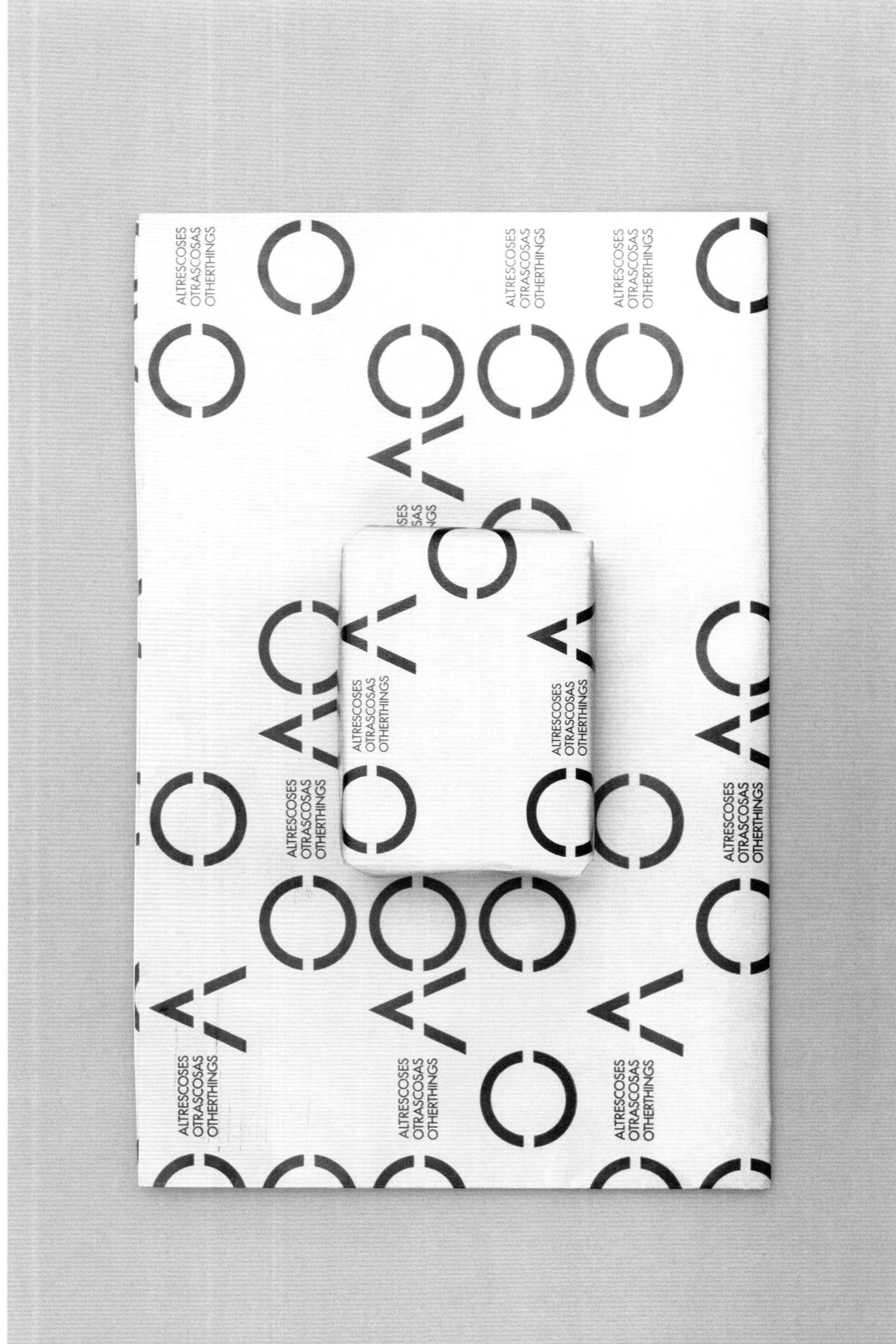

RÍTMIA. MUSIC THERAPY

Identity for social music therapist and educator Celia Castillo. The identity is based on rhythmic exercises developed by Celia with the basic aim of provoking different moods in her patients.

Design Agency: Atipus ***Creative Direction:*** Atipus ***Design:*** Albert Estruch ***Client:*** Celia Castillo. Rítmia

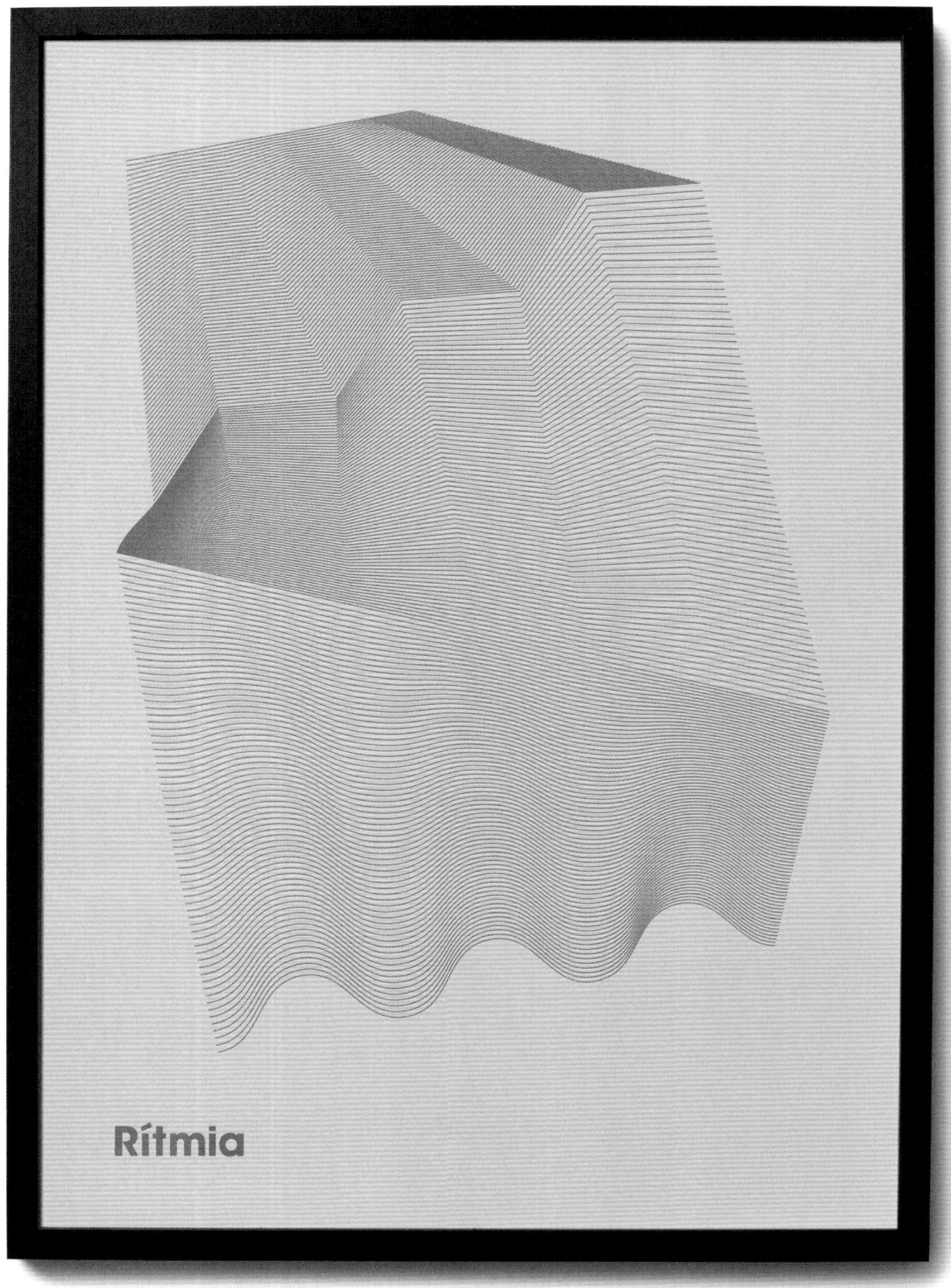
Rítmia

CRYPTOGRAPHER & ENCODED TEXTILES

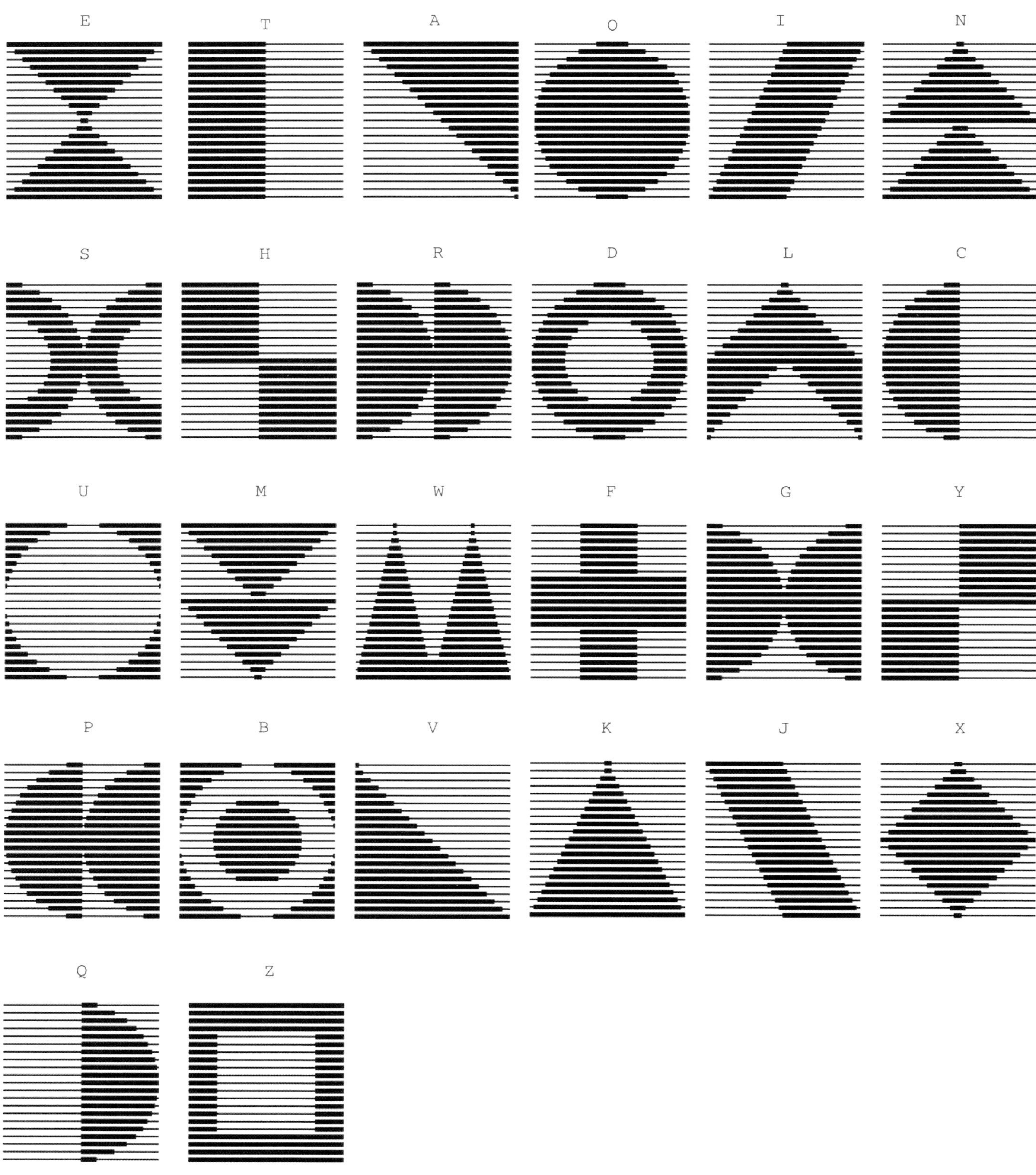

The Cryptographer generates patterns by translating words into code. The process is controlled by text messaging; each texted character is transformed into a specified icon, resulting in ever-changing patterns formed by the user's input. When bleached into fabric, the message's invisible words are given a tangible, physical impact. Bleach is applied by a pen attached to the print head of the Cryptographer. The process reacts differently to each textile dye used, causing the resulting shades to vary. The size and scale of the pattern are determined by the amount of words sent to the printer. The resulting creations are scarves whose patterns are personalized secret messages. Special thanks to collaborators: Remon van den Eijnden, Peter Bust, Bart van der Linden and Studio Watt.

Design Agency: Raw Color

RESIDENCY BRANDING

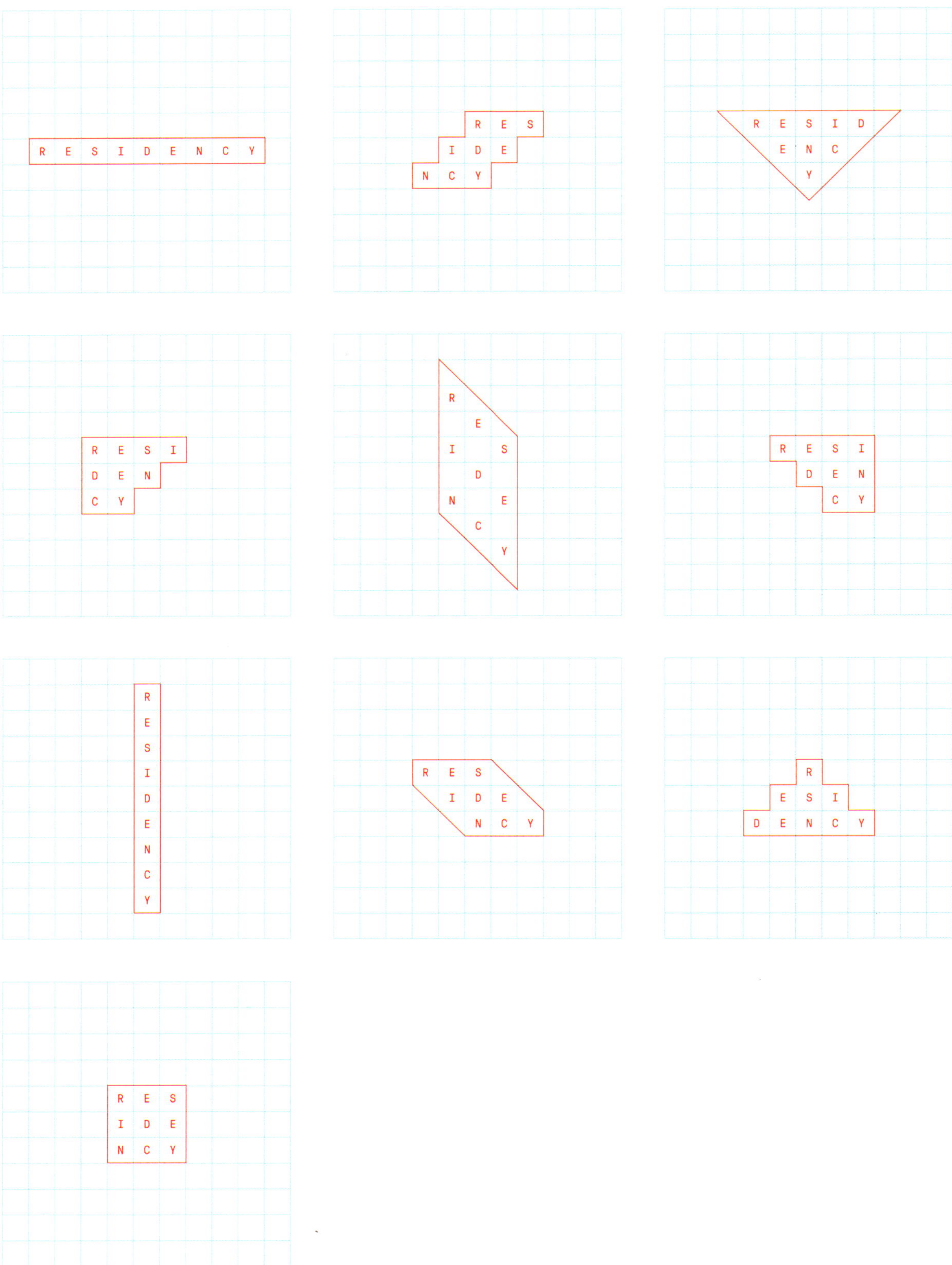

Residency Content is a new production company based in New York, representing a wide pool of talents from different backgrounds. Residency produces music videos, short films, documentaries, and commercials. Jules Tardy was commissioned to design an identity system and a website that reflect the eclectic nature of the brand. The word mark fluctuates when applied across various applications, bringing the identity to life in different shapes both in print and online.

Art Direction: Jules Tardy *Design:* Jules Tardy *Developer:* Phillip Pastore

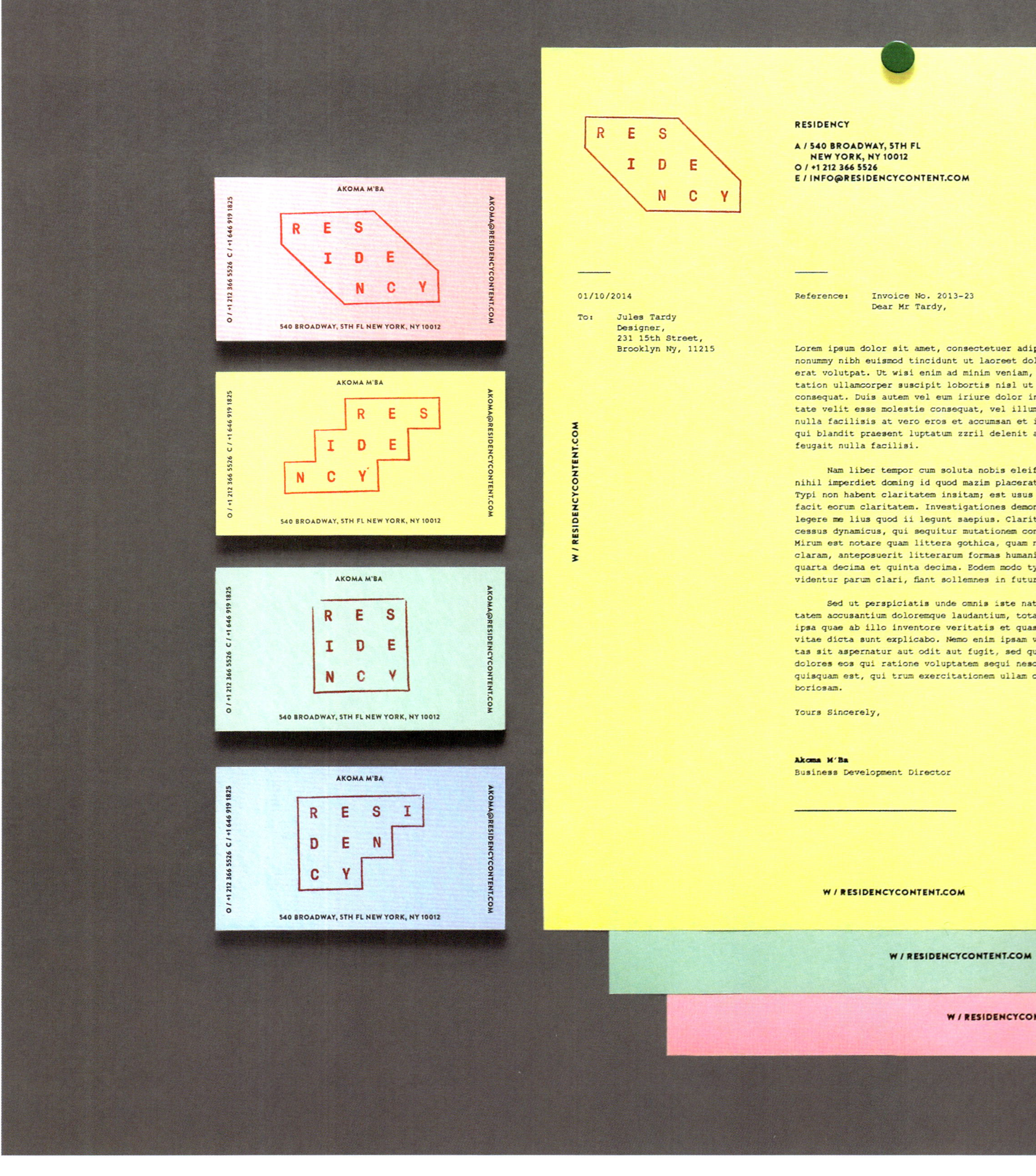
AKOMA M'BA
R E S
I D E
N C Y
540 BROADWAY, 5TH FL NEW YORK, NY 10012
O / +1 212 366 5526 C / +1 646 919 1825
AKOMA@RESIDENCYCONTENT.COM

AKOMA M'BA
R E S
I D E
N C Y
540 BROADWAY, 5TH FL NEW YORK, NY 10012
O / +1 212 366 5526 C / +1 646 919 1825
AKOMA@RESIDENCYCONTENT.COM

AKOMA M'BA
R E S
I D E
N C Y
540 BROADWAY, 5TH FL NEW YORK, NY 10012
O / +1 212 366 5526 C / +1 646 919 1825
AKOMA@RESIDENCYCONTENT.COM

AKOMA M'BA
R E S I
D E N C
C Y
540 BROADWAY, 5TH FL NEW YORK, NY 10012
O / +1 212 366 5526 C / +1 646 919 1825
AKOMA@RESIDENCYCONTENT.COM

R E S
I D E
N C Y

RESIDENCY
A / 540 BROADWAY, 5TH FL
    NEW YORK, NY 10012
O / +1 212 366 5526
E / INFO@RESIDENCYCONTENT.COM

W / RESIDENCYCONTENT.COM

01/10/2014

To: Jules Tardy
       Designer,
       231 15th Street,
       Brooklyn Ny, 11215

Reference: Invoice No. 2013-23
              Dear Mr Tardy,

Lorem ipsum dolor sit amet, consectetuer adipis
nonummy nibh euismod tincidunt ut laoreet dolo
erat volutpat. Ut wisi enim ad minim veniam, qu
tation ullamcorper suscipit lobortis nisl ut al
consequat. Duis autem vel eum iriure dolor in h
tate velit esse molestie consequat, vel illum d
nulla facilisis at vero eros et accumsan et ius
qui blandit praesent luptatum zzril delenit aug
feugait nulla facilisi.

    Nam liber tempor cum soluta nobis eleifen
nihil imperdiet doming id quod mazim placerat x
Typi non habent claritatem insitam; est usus le
facit eorum claritatem. Investigationes demonst
legere me lius quod ii legunt saepius. Claritas
cessus dynamicus, qui sequitur mutationem consu
Mirum est notare quam littera gothica, quam nur
claram, anteposuerit litterarum formas humanita
quarta decima et quinta decima. Eodem modo typi
videntur parum clari, fiant sollemnes in futuru

    Sed ut perspiciatis unde omnis iste natus
tatem accusantium doloremque laudantium, totam
ipsa quae ab illo inventore veritatis et quasi
vitae dicta sunt explicabo. Nemo enim ipsam vol
tas sit aspernatur aut odit aut fugit, sed quia
dolores eos qui ratione voluptatem sequi nesciu
quisquam est, qui trum exercitationem ullam cor
boriosam.

Yours Sincerely,

Akoma M'Ba
Business Development Director

W / RESIDENCYCONTENT.COM

W / RESIDENCYCONTENT.COM

W / RESIDENCYCONT

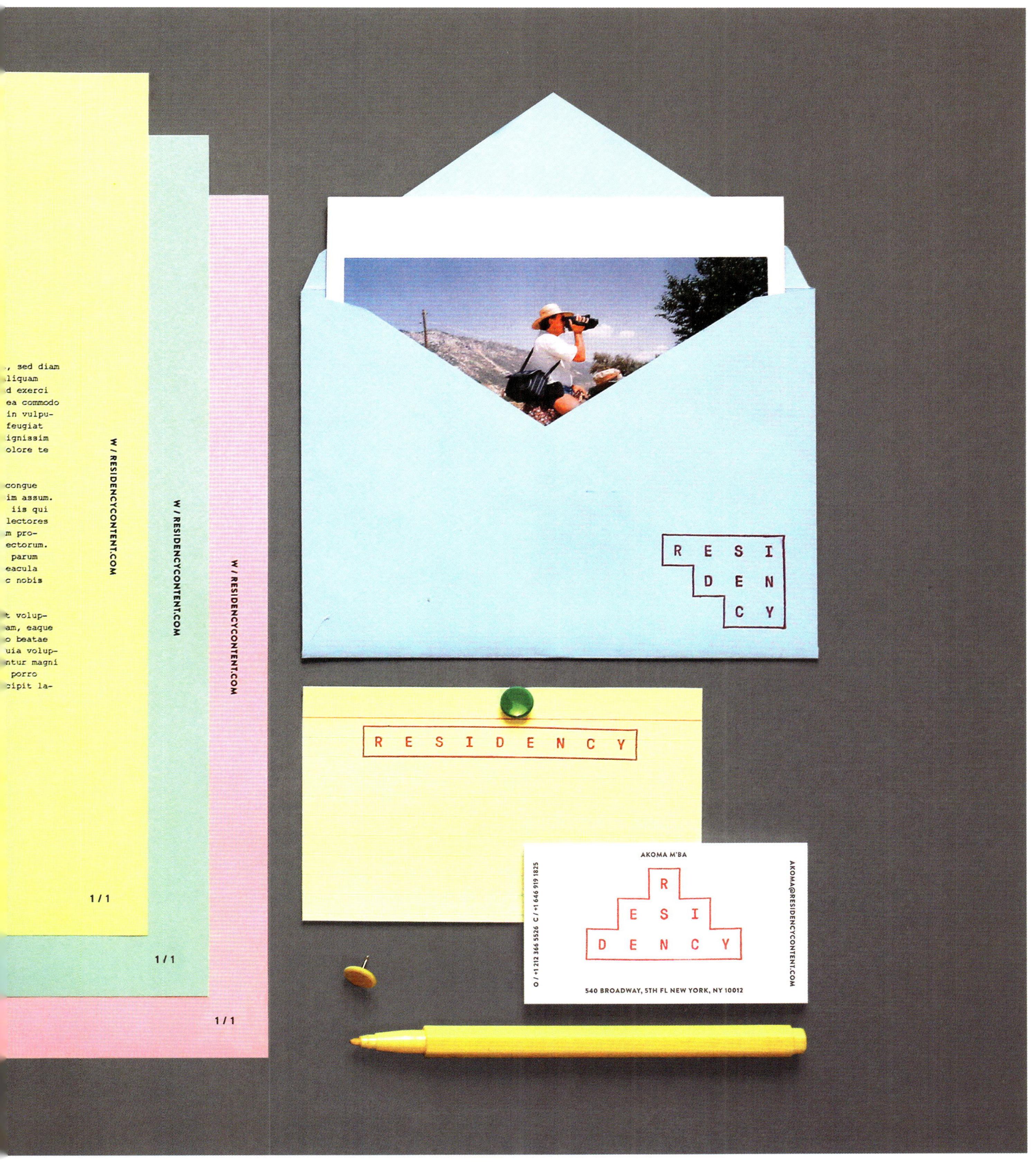
W / RESIDENCYCONTENT.COM
W / RESIDENCYCONTENT.COM
W / RESIDENCYCONTENT.COM
1 / 1
1 / 1
1 / 1
RESIDENCY
RESIDENCY
AKOMA M'BA
O / +1 212 366 5526 C / +1 646 919 1825
AKOMA@RESIDENCYCONTENT.COM
RESIDENCY
540 BROADWAY, 5TH FL NEW YORK, NY 10012

Workshop project for new media and 3D technology. The project includes A1-sized posters and folded fliers.

Design Agency: Anymade Studio **Design:** Petr Cabalka & Filip Nerad **Photography:** Anymade Studio

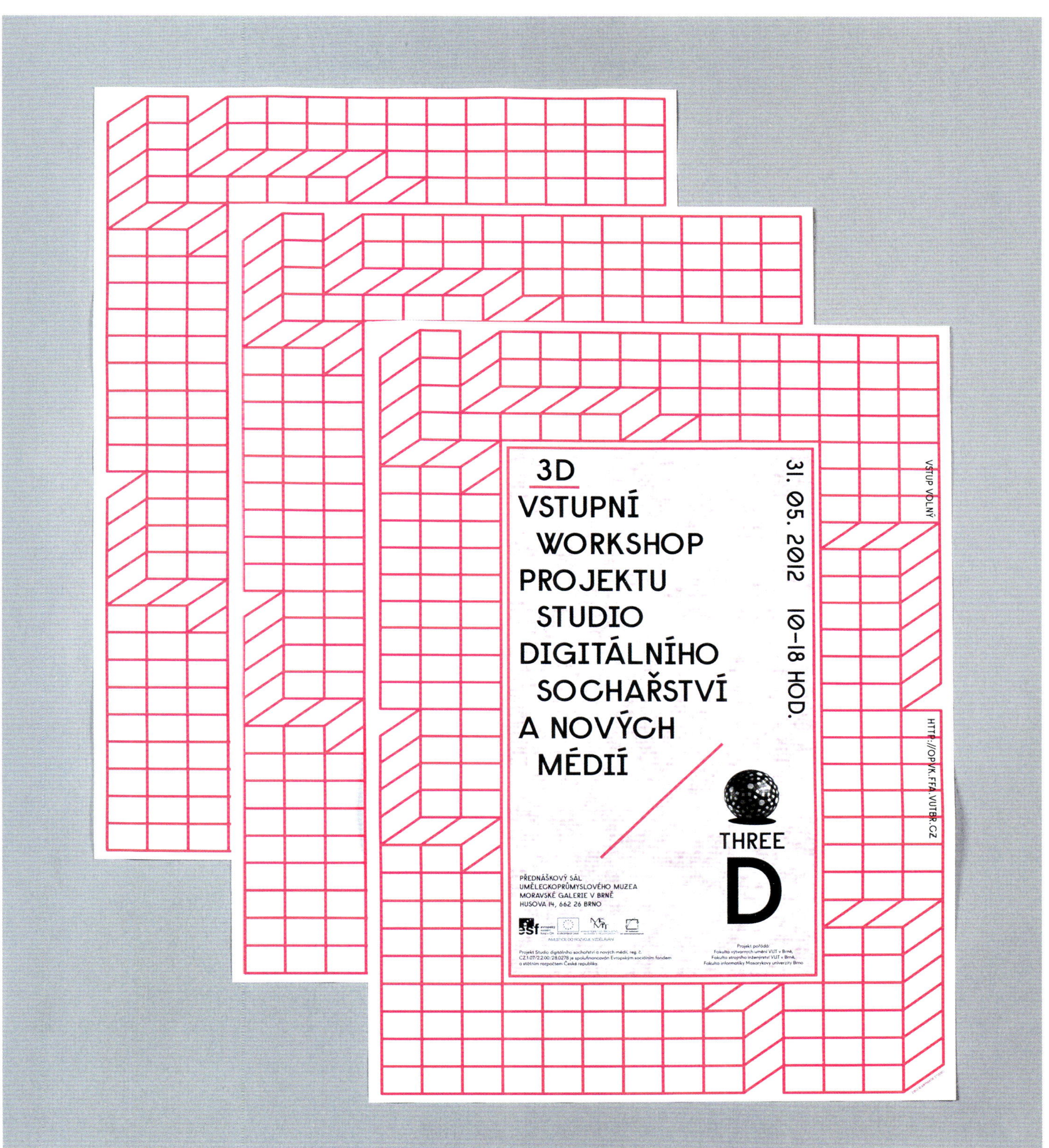

3D
VSTUPNÍ
WORKSHOP
PROJEKTU
STUDIO
DIGITÁLNÍHO
SOCHAŘSTVÍ
A NOVÝCH
MÉDIÍ
31. 05. 2012 10–18 HOD.
VSTUP VOLNÝ
HTTP://OPVK.FFA.VUTBR.CZ
THREE
D
PŘEDNÁŠKOVÝ SÁL
UMĚLECKOPRŮMYSLOVÉHO MUZEA
MORAVSKÉ GALERIE V BRNĚ
HUSOVA 14, 662 26 BRNO
INVESTICE DO ROZVOJE VZDĚLÁVÁNÍ
Projekt Studio digitálního sochařství a nových médií, reg. č.
CZ.1.07/2.2.00/28.0278 je spolufinancován Evropským sociálním fondem
a státním rozpočtem České republiky.
Projekt pořádá:
Fakulta výtvarných umění VUT v Brně,
Fakulta strojního inženýrství VUT v Brně,
Fakulta informatiky Masarykovy univerzity Brno

3D

VSTUPNÍ
WORKSHOP
PROJEKTU
STUDIO
DIGITÁLNÍHO
SOCHAŘSTVÍ
A NOVÝCH
MÉDIÍ

31. 05. 2012

VSTUP VOLNÝ   HTTP://OPVK.FFA.VUTBR.CZ

31. 05. 2012
10–18 HOD.

PŘEDNÁŠKOVÝ SÁL
UMĚLECKOPRŮMYSLOVÉHO MUZEA
MORAVSKÉ GALERIE V BRNĚ
HUSOVA 14, 662 26 BRNO

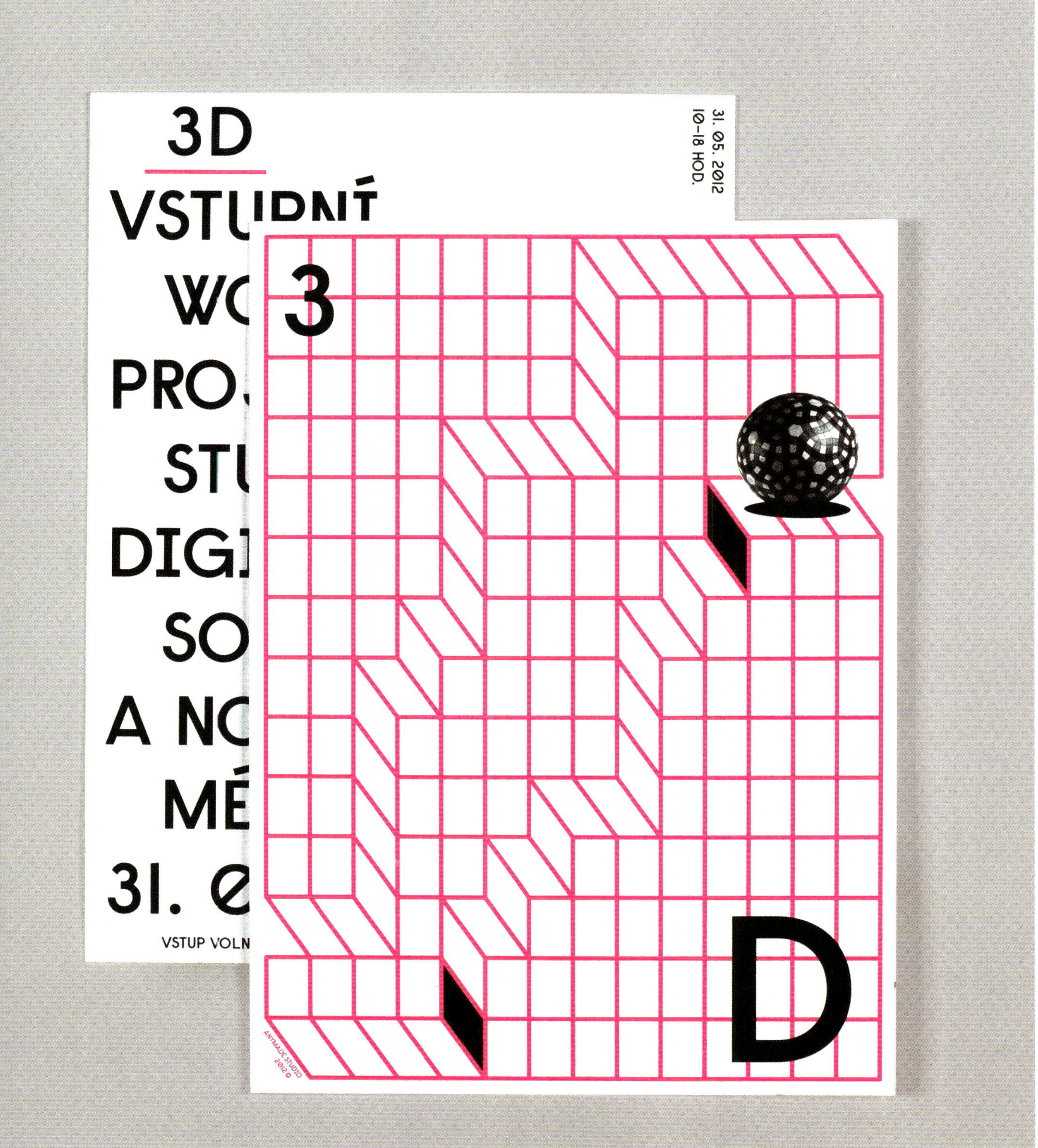
3D
VSTUPNÍ
WO
PRO
STU
DIGI
SO
A NO
MÉ
31. 0
VSTUP VOLN
31. 05. 2012
10–18 HOD.
3
D
ANYMADE STUDIO
© 2012

BOOK, PUBLISHING HOUSE

The logo "Book," created in June 2013 by Maurizio Pagnozzi, is part of a project for a course in graphic design taken by the designer at ILAS, Institute of Communication of Naples.
The strength of the project is entirely expressed by the shape of the letters, depicted in concentric circles that lead the eyes of the observer in a hypnotic game; reading the books published by this publishing house should be a hypnotic experience. The corporate color used is black, a color that recalls elegance, but there is also a special edition in red and gold.

Creative Direction: Maurizio Pagnozzi *Design:* Maurizio Pagnozzi

Lorem ipsum dolor sit amet, consectetur adipiscing elit. Morbi non dapibus tellus. Duis ut rhoncus risus.

NEUROTREND

The key graphic solution for this project was based on the visualizations of medical gear. Following this notion, the corporate identity is filled with bent lines, whose variations helped designers create certain shapes and images rather than chaotic patterns. In most cases, the image is given volume in the physical dimension by embossing the surface.

Art Direction: Vladimir Shlygin *Design:* Vladimir Shlygin & Olga Papsuy *Copyright:* Maxim Pantsyrev

NEUROTREND
DMITRY ELINZON
technical director
+7 (917) 577 57 78 (моб.)
+7 (499) 346 03 23
in@neurotrend.ru
1-st Mozhaisky Tupik 8A bld. 1,
Moscow, Russia, 121059

MUSIC MUSEUM OF BARCELONA

Music, as an abstract concept, is easier to feel and reproduce than to explain. Based on this idea, this project graphically represents music and its elements as if they were a game. Through the museum's attempt to capture the essence of the music, it is transformed into a lively and versatile item, allowing for many variations and applications.

Design: Fredic Barrera

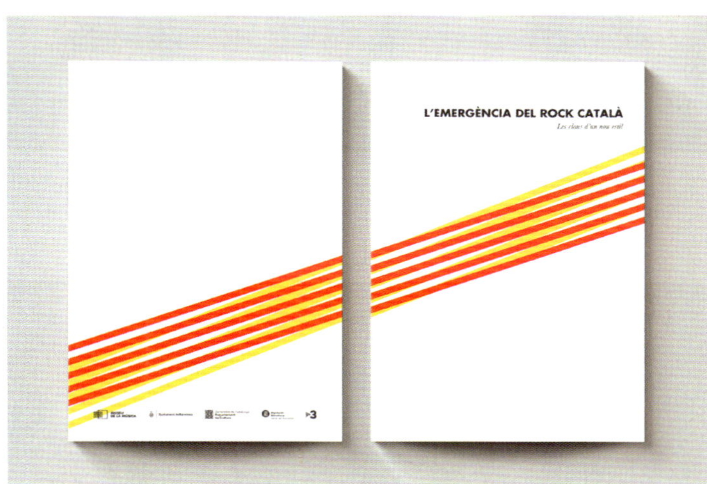

L'EMERGÈNCIA DEL ROCK CATALÀ
Les claus d'un nou estil

L'AUDITORI. C/LEPANT, 150, 2A PL.
08013 · BARCELONA
T. 93 256 36 50
www.museumusica.bcn.cat
MUSEU
DE LA MÚSICA

COTTON CLUB
COTTON CLUB

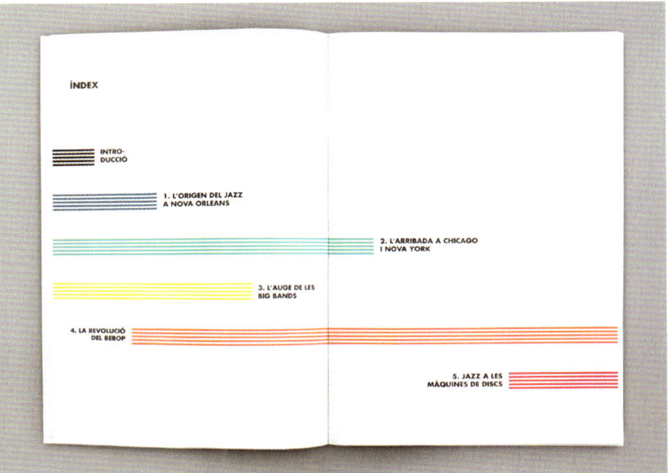

ÍNDEX
INTRO-
DUCCIÓ
1. L'ORIGEN DEL JAZZ
A NOVA ORLEANS
2. L'ARRIBADA A CHICAGO
I NOVA YORK
3. L'AUGE DE LES
BIG BANDS
4. LA REVOLUCIÓ
DEL BEBOP
5. JAZZ A LES
MÀQUINES DE DISCS

HOTEL FOMF

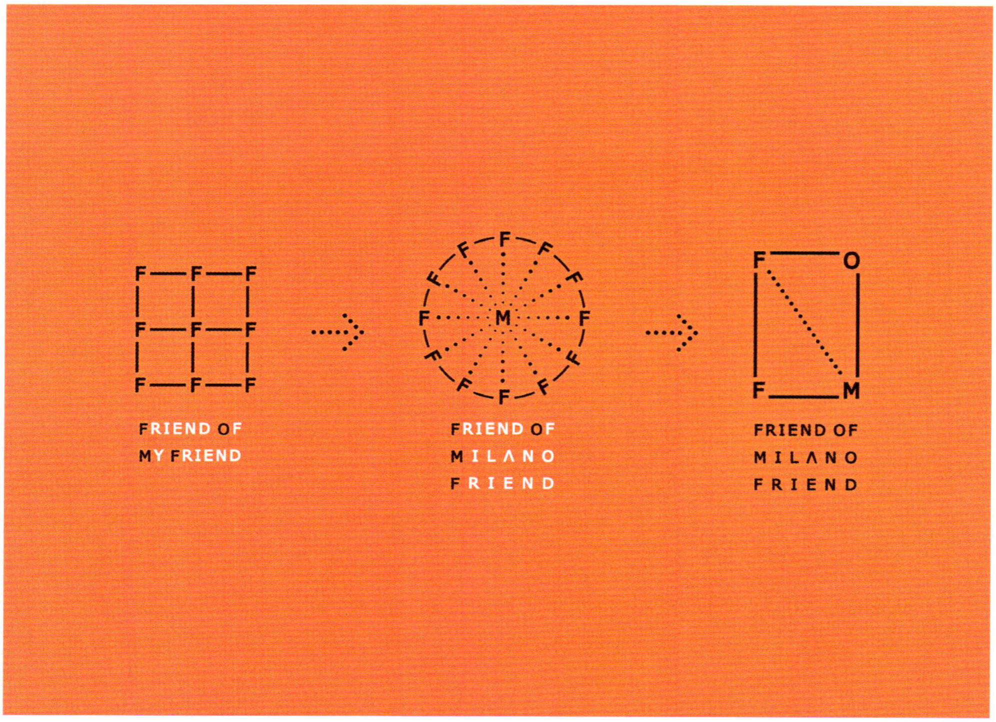

The inspiration for this project came from a term commonly used in cities, "friend-of-a-friend." The idea was to create an experience that would inspire customers to feel as if they were thinking of a friend in Milan when thinking about this new Milan-based hotel. After experiencing the casual but still respectful atmosphere, customers would tell their friends, who in turn would tell their own friends. When the word was out, it would be like friends from every corner of the world were gathering in this hotel in Milan.

Art Direction: Ray Yen *Design:* Ray Yen

DELAFÉ Y LAS FLORES AZULES

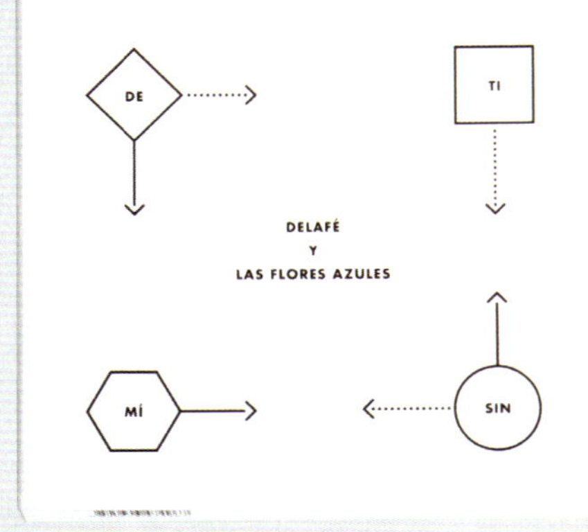

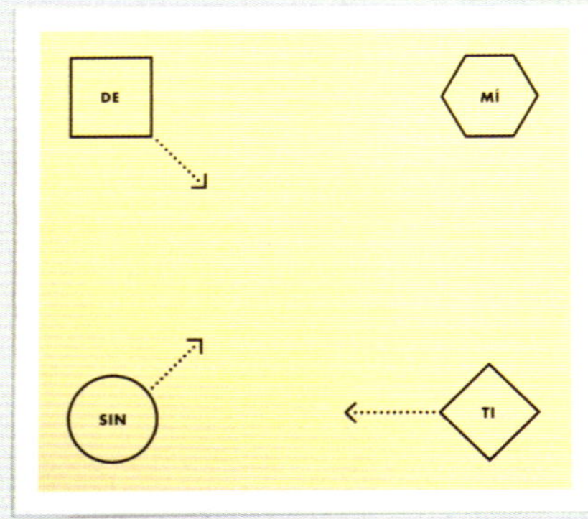

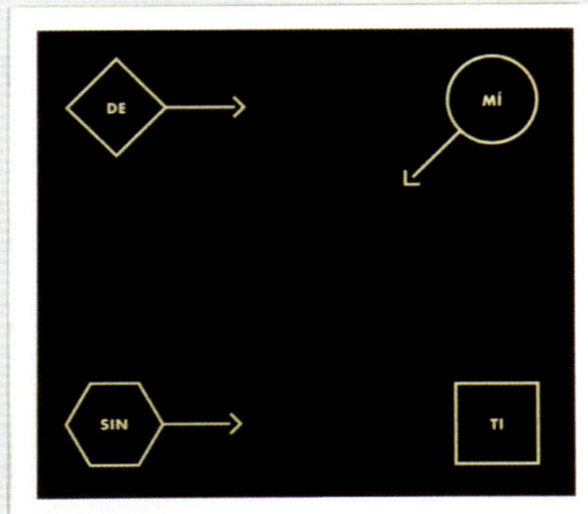

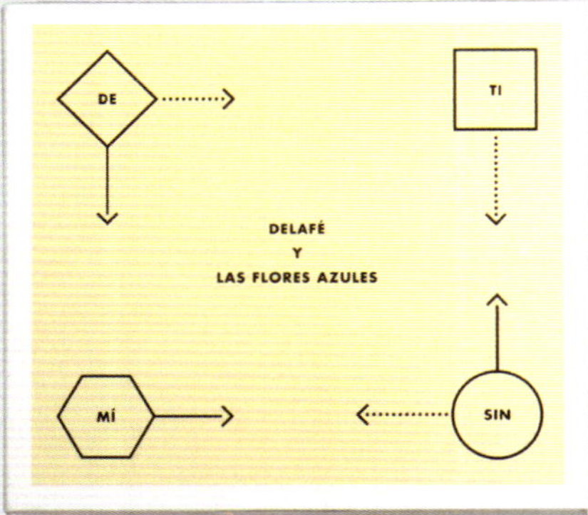

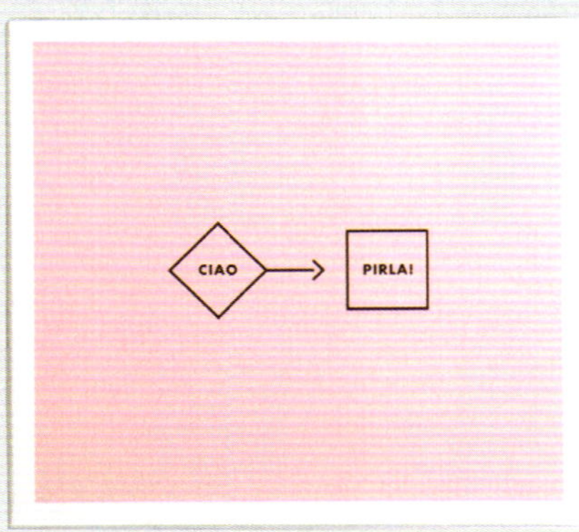

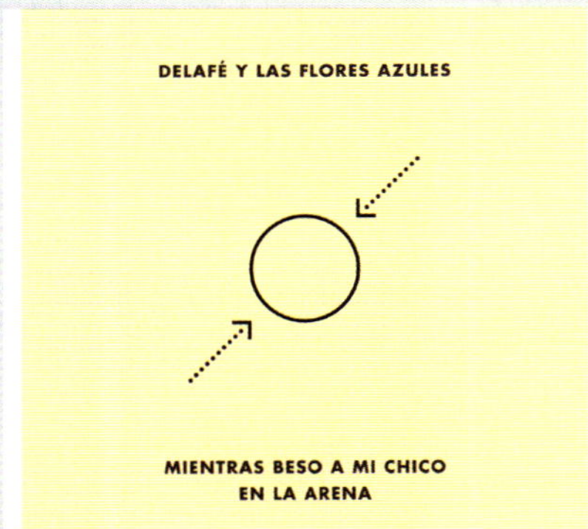

Artwork for the new album, "Delafé y las Flores Azules." The system was created for all of their communication elements.

Design Agency: Opisso Studio ***Art Direction:*** Opisso Studio

Brighton Road Studios provides collaborative work spaces for diverse creatives, from fine artists to photographers and architects. The identity features a "B," formed out of various combinations of geometric shapes and colors, representing the creative possibilities that result from different disciplines sharing space, ideas, and working collaboratively. Although the logo appears in hundreds of combinations, the core look and feel of the branding remains distinctive.

Design Agency: Glad **Creative Direction:** David Burdon

MÁ DA FITA IDENTITY

Considering Má da Fita's identity as a documentary team, their personal vision is shared through their recordings of other people's narratives. Royal took this notion one step further and focused on how communication develops to empower narratives and feeds into specific ambiences when designing their logo. In order to make Má da Fita's brand a tool for narration, Royal searched for the parallels between the environment of multimedia and that of identity. The brand is composed of three physical elements, as well as printed and digital objects designed to seem incomplete and the printed objects that complete them. Má da Fita's visual identity thus became a story-telling device, documenting their identity much in the way an interview records content that poetically engages with an individual's background.

Design Agency: Royal Studio **Client:** Má da Fita

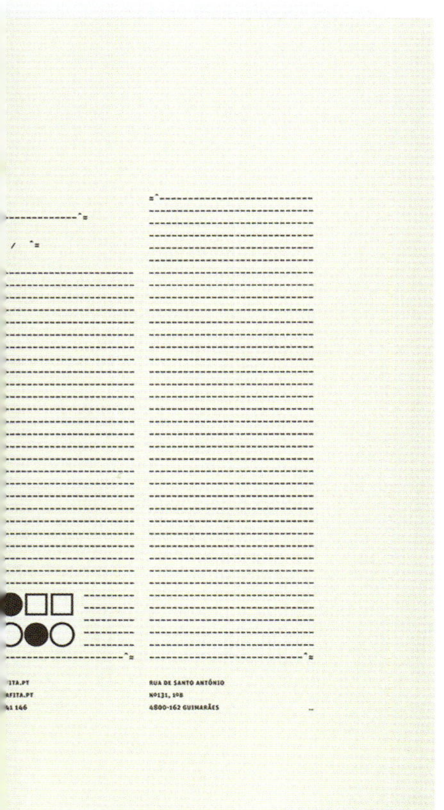

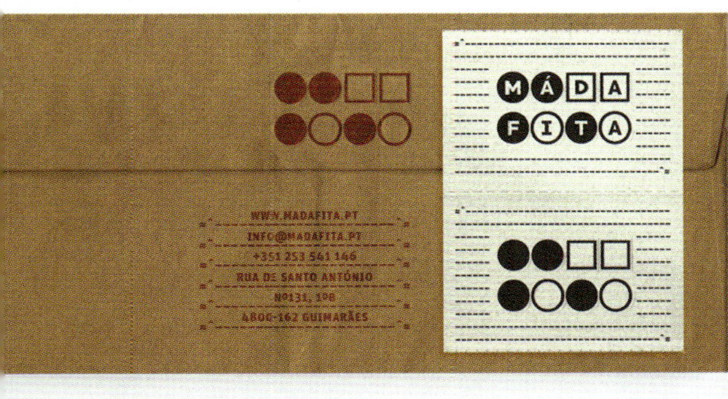

MÁDA FITA
WWW.MADAFITA.PT
INFO@MADAFITA.PT
+351 253 541 146
RUA DE SANTO ANTÓNIO
Nº131, 1ºB
4800-162 GUIMARÃES

MÁDA FITA
WWW.MADAFITA.PT
INFO@MADAFITA.PT
+351 253 541 146
RUA DE SANTO ANTÓNIO
Nº131, 1ºB
4800-162 GUIMARÃES

TIN CAN

TIN CAN is a Dutch production company that focuses on the development and production of projects in the field of television, branding, online and events.

As is shown, the entire identity consists of two basic elements that constitute the logo; a basic typography and four basic lines. Each line refers to one of the four disciplines of their profession. These lines are the main "format" for the entire identity and are adaptable to different types of content and applications.

Design Agency: COOEE

format
content
product
A TIN CAN
4 DISCIPLINES
TELEVISION
IDENTIT
TIN
WRAPPING CONTENT
WRAPPING CONTENT
INTERIOR
typography
4 lines
TWO BASICS
OBJECTS
ONE TOOLBOX
TIN CAN
ALL IN ONE LOGO

TINCAN.NL

eten &
drinken
eten &
drinken

EVO – BACK TO BASICS

In the midst of the economic crisis, Evo Bank wanted to prove that banks can put their customers first by placing their interests directly into its business model. Evo offers one single and simple product that integrates a traditional savings account with a current account, which dynamically feed one another to deliver the greatest possible return to the account holder — an evolved banking model for a new context.

Design Agency: Saffron *Client:* NovaCaixaGalicia Bank

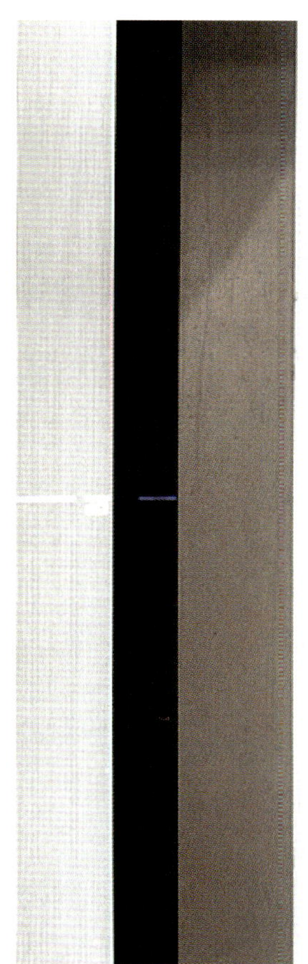

EVO

EVO
BANCA INTELIGENTE
EVO
EVO
EVO
CUENTA INTELIGENTE EVO.
TAN DIFERENTE QUE HEMOS TENIDO
QUE LANZAR TODO UN BANCO
PARA VENDERLA.

GEOMETREEK

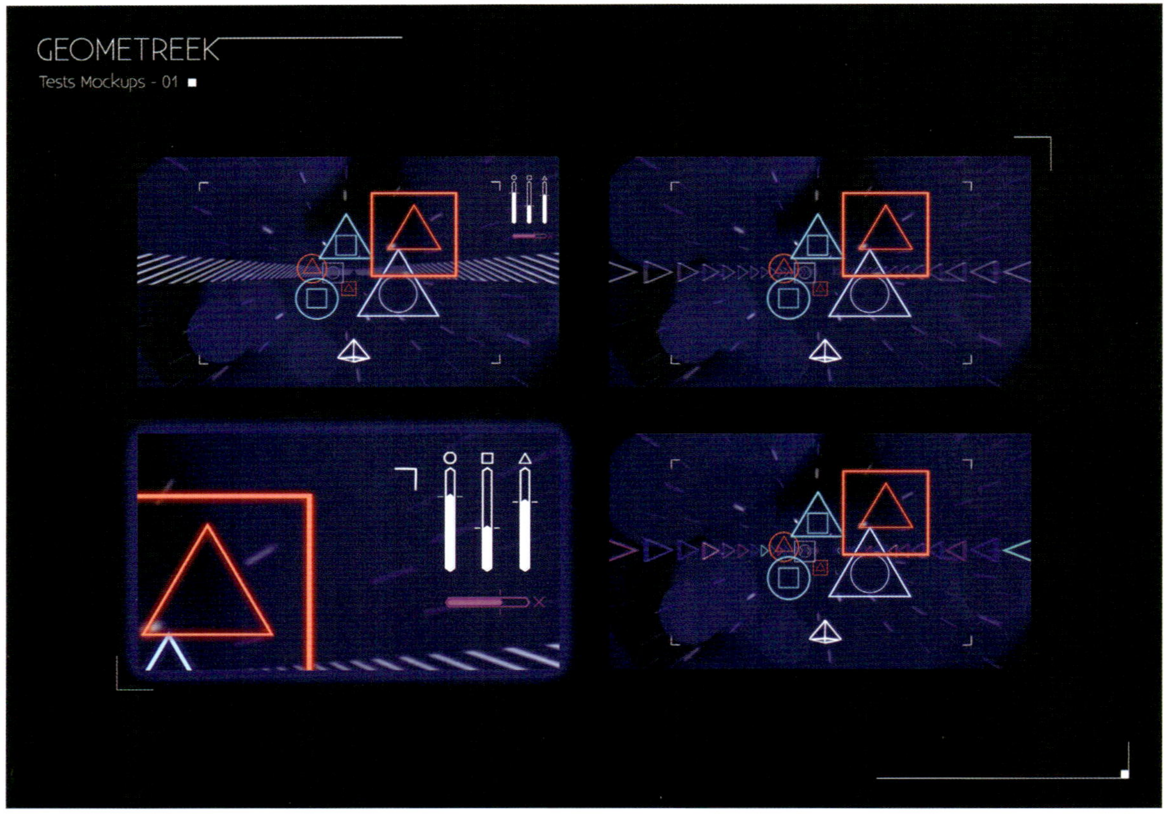

Concept and logo design for "Geometreek," a 3D game project. The aim of the game is to left-click to change the cursor's shape so it matches the next geometric shape approaching in order to pass through it. The pace of level is set by changing musical tracks. What you see here is the first visual research for the game.

Design Agency: FLAT226 ***3D Animator & Concept:*** Yannick Jouneau ***2D Graphic Designer:*** Margot Madranges

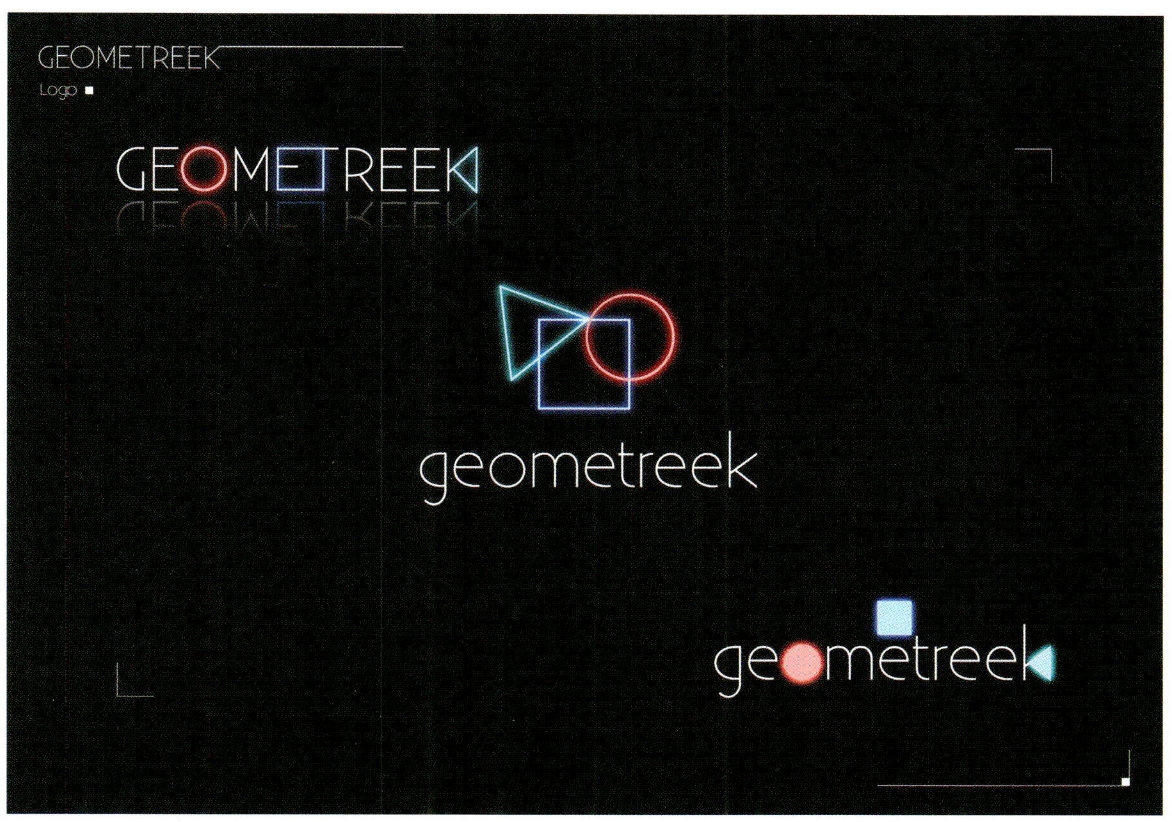
GEOMETREEK
geometreek
geometreek

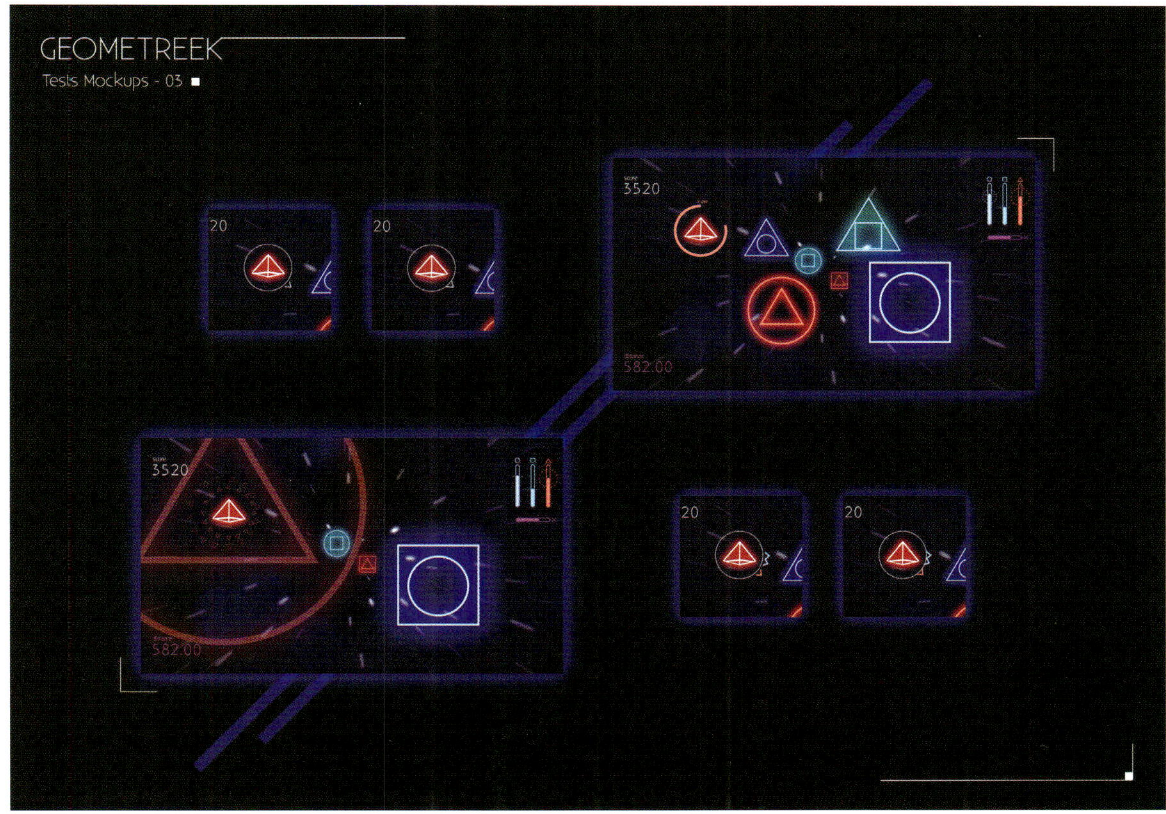

LITTLE PRINCE MUSEUM VISUAL IDENTITY

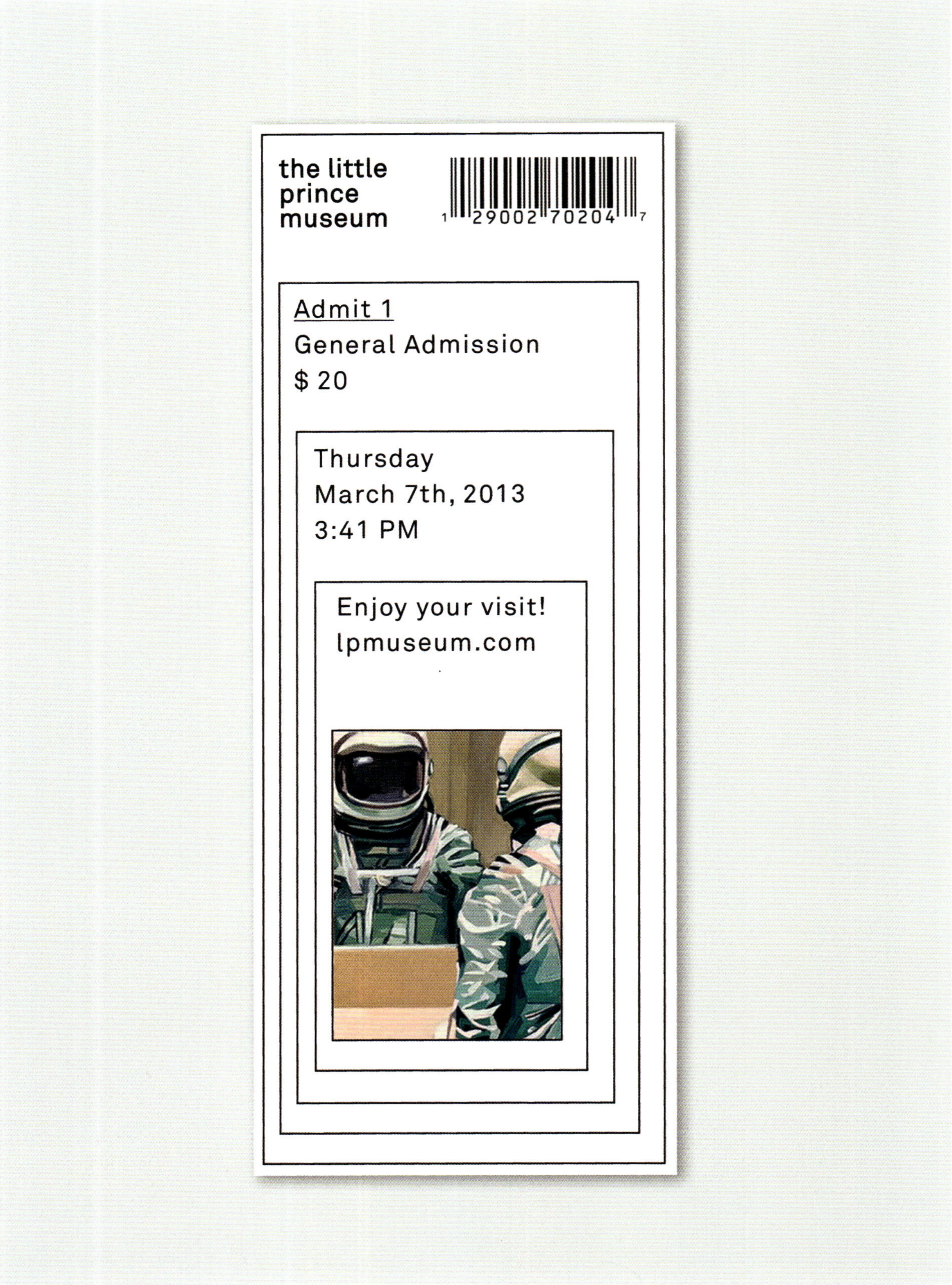

The Little Prince Museum is a fictitious museum of art and design that showcases Surrealist works from all over the world.
The museum is named after *The Little Prince* book, by Antoine De Saint-Exupery, in honor of the book's surrealist plot and fantastical illustrations.
The museum's minimalist style and lines are intended to contrast with the natural shapes of the rocky mountains of the desert, similar to the Surrealist art exposed in the museum.

Design: Leo Porto *Instruction:* Natasha Jen

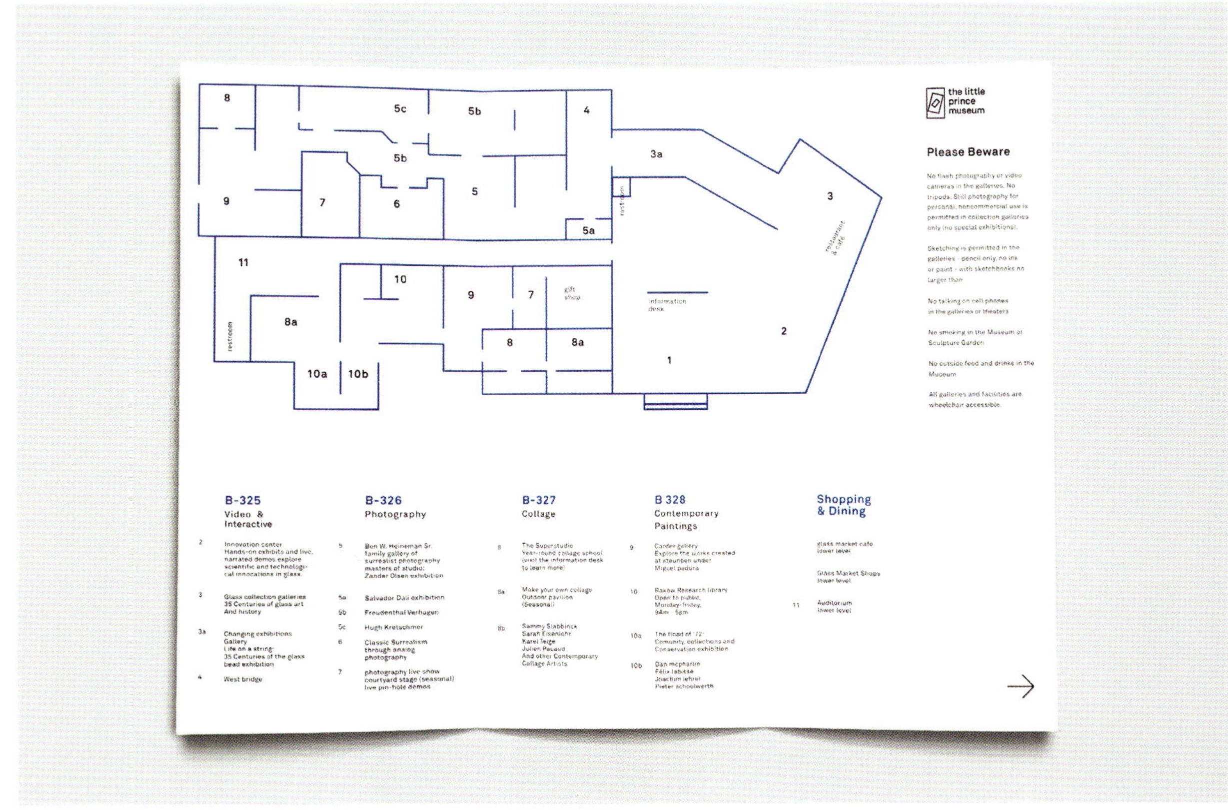

the little prince museum

Please Beware

No flash photography or video
cameras in the galleries. No
tripods. Still photography for
personal, noncommercial use is
permitted in collection galleries
only (no special exhibitions).

Sketching is permitted in the
galleries - pencil only, no ink
or paint - with sketchbooks no
larger than

No talking on cell phones
in the galleries or theaters

No smoking in the Museum or
Sculpture Garden

No outside food and drinks in the
Museum

All galleries and facilities are
wheelchair accessible.

B-325
Video &
Interactive

2   Innovation center
    Hands-on exhibits and live,
    narrated demos explore
    scientific and technologi-
    cal innovations in glass.

3   Glass collection galleries
    35 Centuries of glass art
    And history

3a Changing exhibitions
    Gallery
    Life on a string:
    35 Centuries of the glass
    bead exhibition

4   West bridge

B-326
Photography

5   Ben W. Heineman Sr.
    family gallery of
    surrealist photography
    masters of studio:
    Zander Olsen exhibition

5a Salvador Dali exhibition
5b Freudenthal Verhagen
5c Hugh Kretschmer
6   Classic Surrealism
    through analog
    photography
7   photography live show
    courtyard stage (seasonal)
    live pin-hole demos

B-327
Collage

8   The Superstudio
    Year-round collage school
    (visit the information desk
    to learn more)

8a Make your own collage
    Outdoor pavilion
    (Seasonal)

8b Sammy Slabbinck
    Sarah Eisenlohr
    Karel Teige
    Julien Pacaud
    And other Contemporary
    Collage Artists

B 328
Contemporary
Paintings

9   Carder gallery
    Explore the works created
    at steunben under
    Miguel padura

10 Rakow Research library
    Open to public,
    Monday-friday,
    9Am - 5pm

10a The flood of '72'
    Comunity, collections and
    Conservation exhibition

10b Dan mcpharlin
    Félix labisse
    Joachim lehrer
    Pieter schoolwerth

Shopping
& Dining

    glass market cafe
    lower level

    Glass Market Shops
    lower level

11 Auditorium
    lower level

rooftop
gallery
B-365

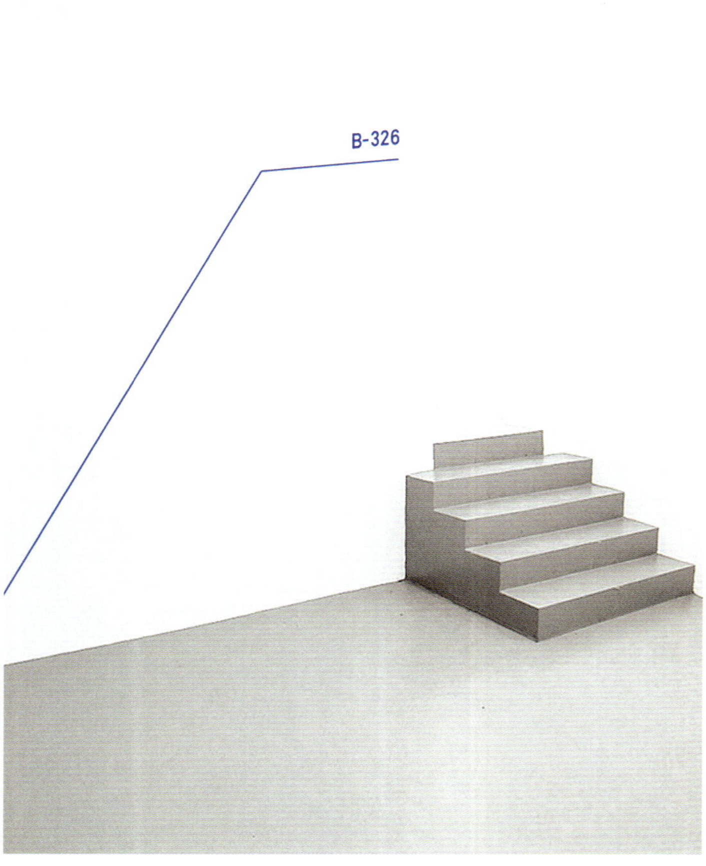

B-326

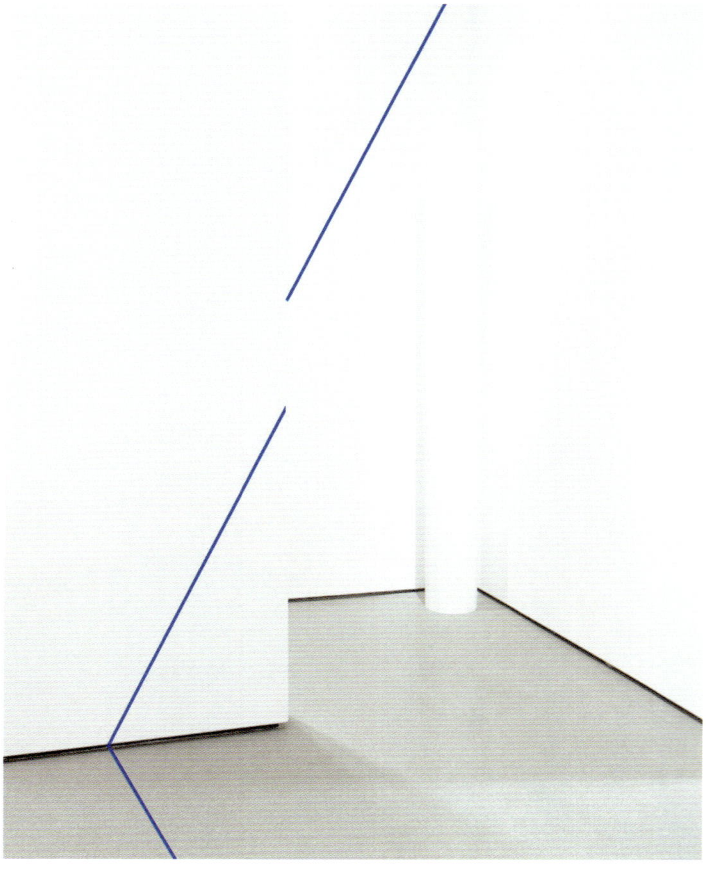

MATCH EXHIBITION

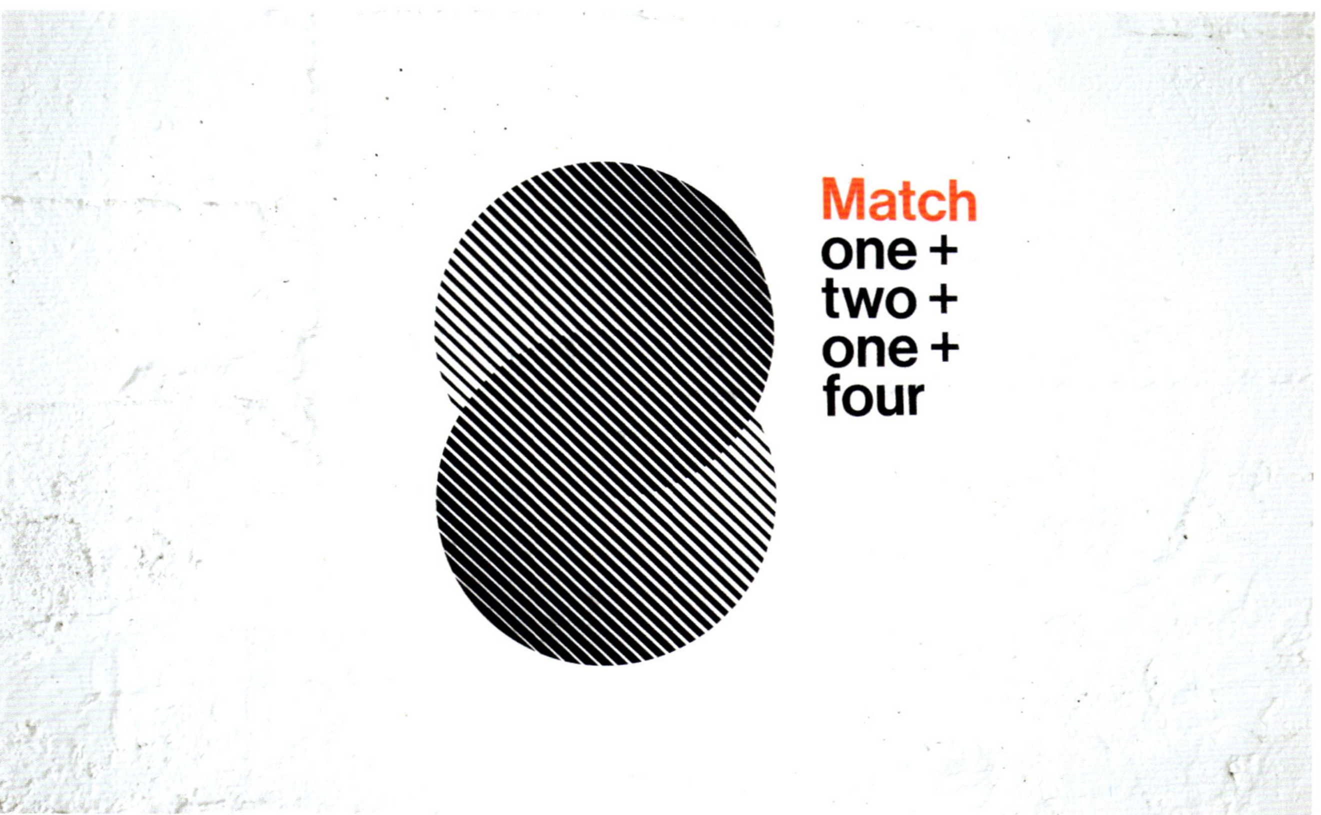

An exhibition for eight photographers who are part of a collective called Match Photographers. The exhibition was an event to showcase the personal works of the photographers to the creative industry, particularly advertising agencies. The graphics generated represent the coming together of the photographers and the agencies in their creative endeavors.

Design Agency: Brogen Averill Studio *Design:* Brogen Averill

Match
one +
one +
six
Match
photographers.
com

Match
one +
three +
four
Match
photographers.
com

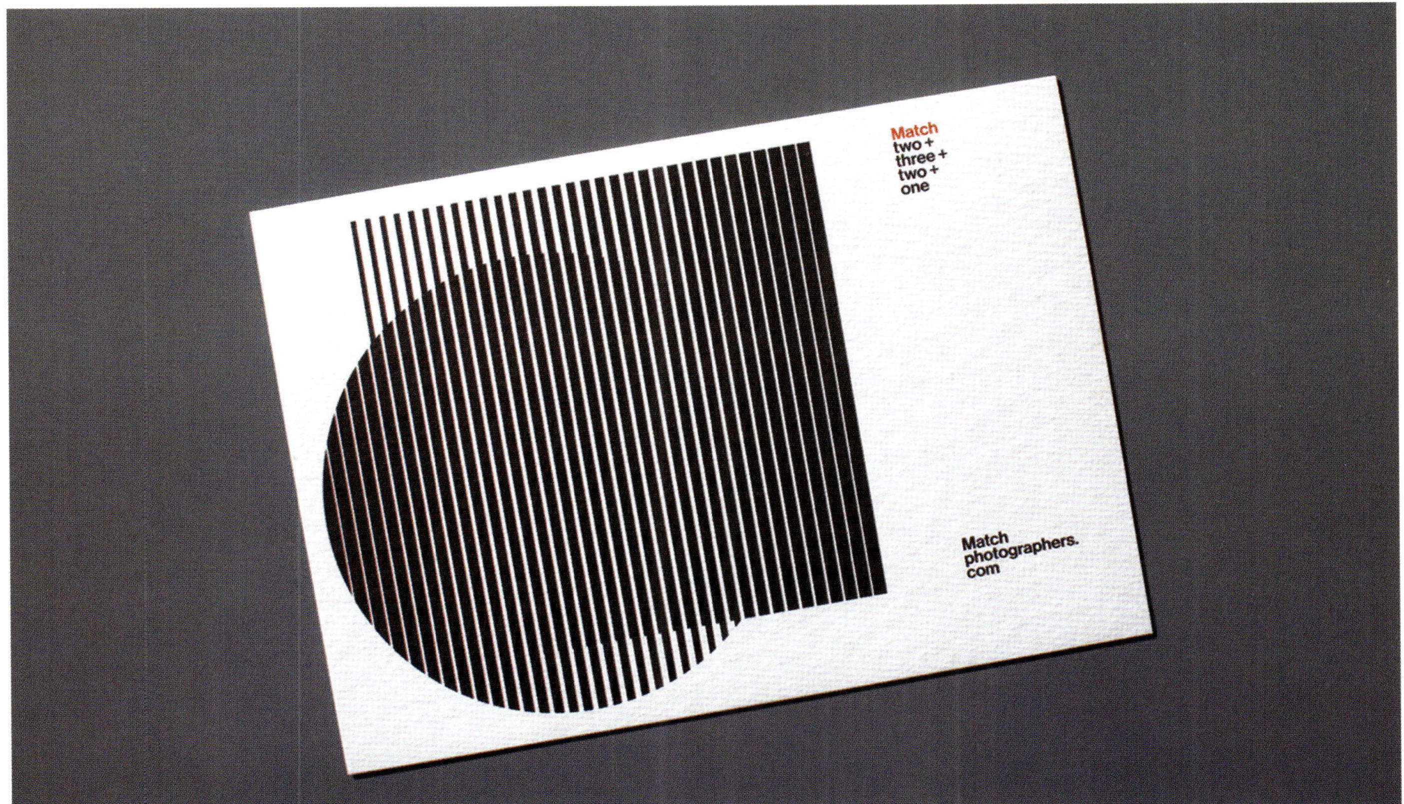
Match
two +
three +
two +
one
Match
photographers.
com

GOLD FOILED NOTEBOOKS

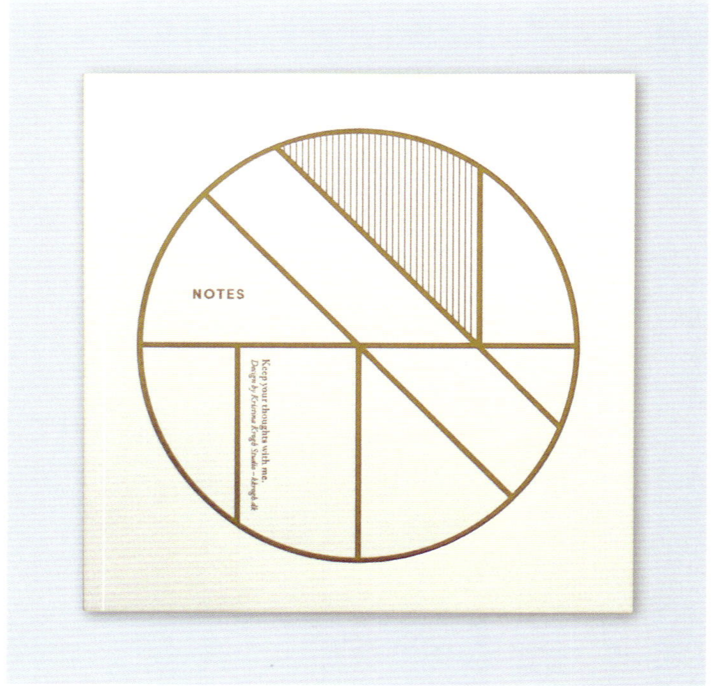

Grey or beige notebooks with gold foil embossing on the covers. The notebooks are 17 x 17 cm with 48 blank white pages and short quotes on the covers, such as "share your ideas and stories with me."

Design Agency: Krogh Studio **Design:** Kristina Krogh

NOTES

AMBIÊNCIA

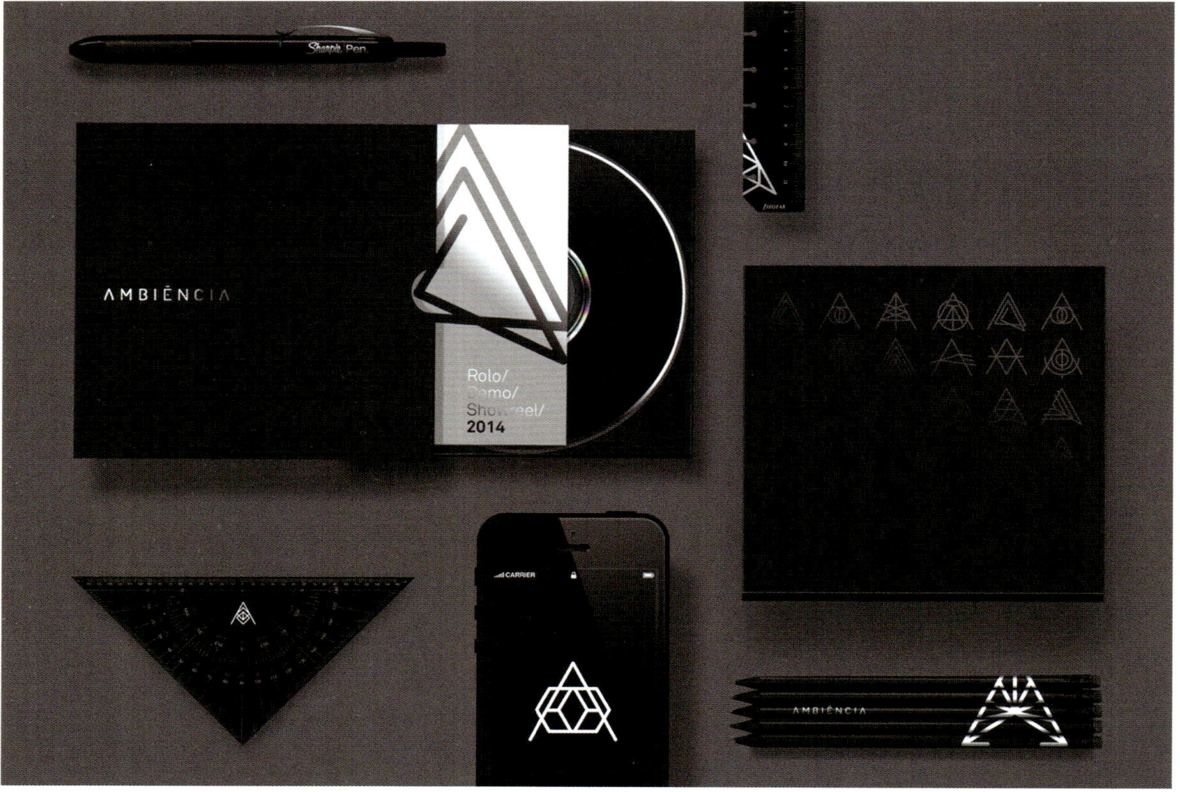

Brand identity project using a dynamic system that incorporates various symbols as graphic elements.

Design Agency: Soulcraft Studio **Design:** Nelson Balaban

AMBIÈNCIA
ambiencia.tv

UNSW 60TH ANNIVERSARY IDENTITY

Identity and related material for the celebratory dinner for 60th anniversary of the University of New South Wales.

Design: Paul Garbett & Elise Santangelino **Client:** the University of New South Wales

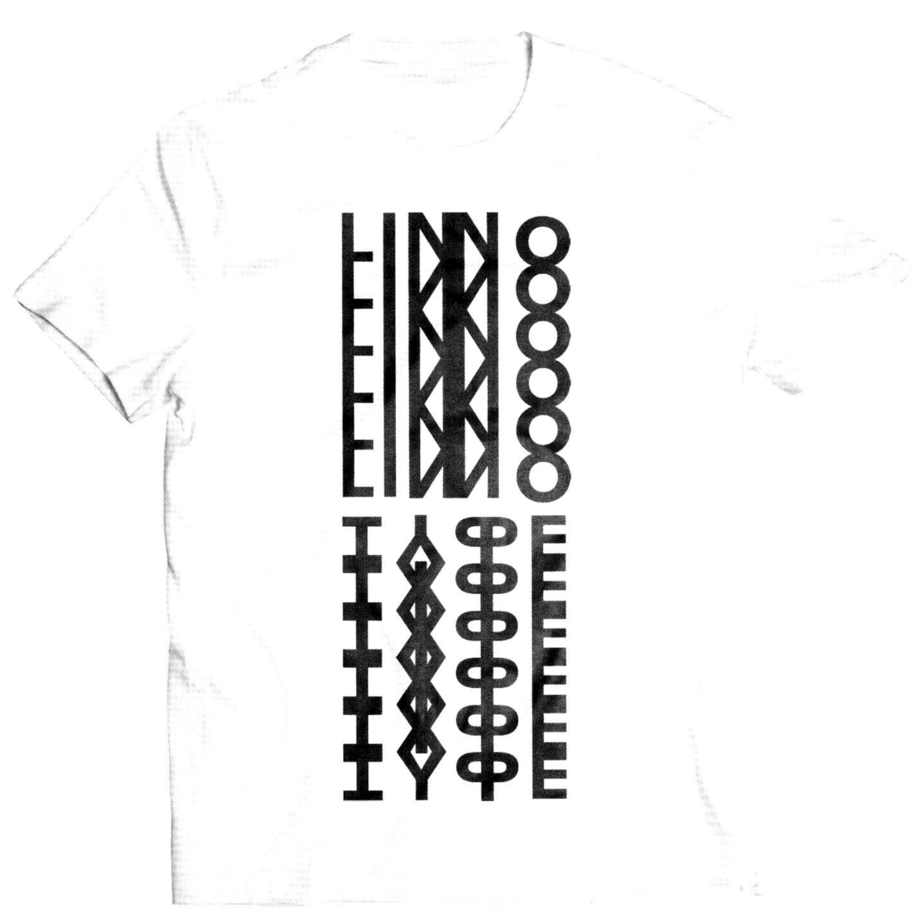

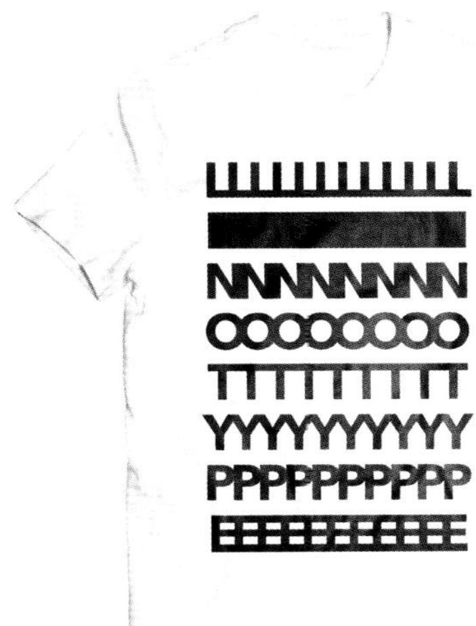

A series of fresh, clean, black and white typographic t-shirts for Linotype. For more than 100 years, the Linotype name has been synonymous with high quality typefaces. They provide superior quality typographic products with a wide range of libraries and font foundries.

Design: Marcel Häusler

INDEX

AIMILIOS GKALIPIS P162-163

Aimilios Gkalipis was born in Australia in 1990 and and still lives in his hometown of Edessa. He studied Graphic Design at the AKTO College and is carrying on his studies at the Middlesex University. He has taken part in exhibitions as well as contests where he has won significant international distinctions. At the moment he works as a freelancer experimenting with graphics and different techniques.
www.bannedgraphics.com

ALEKSANDRA GUDYMENKO P138-139

Aleksandra Gudymenko is a Russia-based designer. She graduated from Saint Petersburg Polytechnic University, faculty of information technologies in design, specializing in graphic design. She currently works as a freelancer.
www.behance.net/alexgud

ALEXANDER EGGER P044-045

Alexander Egger is a graphic designer, illustrator, concept developer, artist, writer, musician and publisher of artzines. Originating from an Italian border area, he is interested in self-imposed limits, open systems, cultural diversity, social interaction, multidimensional communication, moving viewpoints and the potential of conflicts. He is currently living and working in Berlin and sometimes elsewhere.
www.alexanderegger.com

AMRITA MARINO P062-065

Amrita Marino is a Brooklyn-based designer who works in the area of identity and editorial design and enjoys illustration on the side.
www.amritamarino.com

ANNE HELLMAN VOLD P090-091

Anne Hellman Vold is a designer and art director, living and working in Stockholm, Sweden.
www.annehellmanvold.com

ANTI P178-181

Anti is a multi-disciplinary agency offering creative solutions to clients from every part of the world. They believe in simplicity, storytelling, and creating fans.
A passionate story will lead to the sharing of authentic experiences and passions between a client and brand. These experiences in turn will recruit fans. Fans create financial opportunities. With the growing competition for clients' attention, the brands that can secure strong concepts with bold visual signatures are the number one brands of tomorrow.
www.anti.as

ANYMADE STUDIO P198-201

Anymade Studio was founded in 2007 in the Czech Republic. During past years the studio evolved into a multifunctional platform whose activities combine various genres and fields, such as art direction, illustration, graphic design, photography, typography, video, and motion design. Anymade Studio members are Petr Cabalka, Filip Nerad and Jan Šrámek aka VJ Kolouch.
www.anymadestudio.com

JIYONG AHN (AKA ANZI) P164-165

Korean designer Jiyong Ahn, also known as Anzi, is a graphic designer currently working at Studio AOAO as an Art Director.
www.anzioculus.com

ASCEND STUDIO P132-133

Ascend Studio is an independent branding, graphic design and web design agency based in central London. They have a methodical approach of research, positioning, strategy and graphic communication.
This process allows them to have a clear thought that gets to the heart of a brand's true potential, enabling them to create relevant communications that genuinely reflect a brand's true values and their client's objectives.
www.ascendstudio.co.uk

ATIPUS P188-191

Atipus is a graphic communication studio, created in Barcelona in 1998, with a deliberate aim to communicate through good graphic work, conceptually and simply. They are a team of expert professionals trained in various disciplines; corporate identity, art direction, packaging design and web services.
http://www.atipus.com

APPLOVE P026-027

Applove consists of art directors/graphic designers Mia Natt och Dag and Biola Kadiri. Together they form a team with over 10 years of experience in the graphic design field.
www.applove.se

BLOW P182-183

BLOW is a Hong Kong based design studio founded by a renowned young designer, Ken Lo, in 2010. Specialized in branding, identities, packaging, environmental graphics, print, publications and website design, they provide clients with mind-blowing design with simple and bold techniques that helps brands to stand out from the crowd.
www.blow.hk

BROGEN AVERILL STUDIO *P060-061; P226-227*

Brogen Averill Studio was established in 2004. The influence of European design culture and tradition has influenced their work, which is applied to a diverse range of mediums, including: brand and identity development, packaging, print, editorial, signage, way finding systems and website design and development. They create concept lead design, investigating requirements and translating them into solutions that are intelligent, creatively inspiring and ultimately different.
http://www.brogenaverill.com

BVD *P146-147; P152*

BVD is a design and branding agency specialized in strategic design. Together with their clients, BVD moves brands and makes them innovative, sustainable and continuously profitable. BVD believes design is a powerful strategic tool and a successful project does not only require exceptional creativity, but also thoughtful analysis, a high level of business orientation and in-depth knowledge of market conditions. Through the years they have delivered a vast number of successful design projects for leading global brands with outstanding, measurable results.
http://bvd.se/

CATKIN PRITCHARD *P128-129*

Catkin Pritchard is an illustrator and Designer originally from the sunny Isle of Wight, England. She studied graphic design at the University of Plymouth, then began working as part of Herschel Supply's in-house design team in Vancouver, Canada.
http://www.behance.net/catkinpritchard

CHARLES DAOUD *P008-011*

Charles Daoud is a multidisciplinary graphic designer based in Montréal, Canada. He pursues his ongoing quest for visual perfection with undeniable passion. After 15 years in the design industry and numerous international awards, it was his typeface "Dense" that really put Charles on the map. Though he touches almost every aspect of design, his specialties lie in branding, art direction, as well as typeface and web design. His clients range from local print shops to international giants.
www.charlesdaoud.com

CLARA FERNANDEZ *P068-069*

Clara Fernandez is a young graphic designer currently working as a freelance designer. Focused on branding, editorial design, and all kinds of print design, she relishes working on disciplines such as illustration and typography. Clara's work is inspired by her passion for purity, simplicity and clean structured design.
https://www.behance.net/cla

CODE STUDIO *P168*

Code Studio design studio was founded in 2009 in Novosibirsk by Alexander Smirnov and Alexander Pavlenok. They do website and application design as well as develop logos, corporate IDs and print work. Their philosophy is based around the fact that only simple and clever design can be beautiful. They also believe that the core of any project is the idea, but when the idea is implemented in a wrong way it loses the meaning. They insist on staying true to their own style and look for customers who share their values.
http://codestudio.org/

COOEE *P214-217*

COOEE is an Amsterdam-based studio founded in 2010 and run by Leon Dijkstra, who specializes in visual communication with a strong focus on publication design and visual identities. In this way, he provides organizations and brands ways to define and visualize their story and image.
http://cooee.nl/

DAVIDE DI GENNARO & ILARIA TOMAT *P124-127*

David Di Gennaro: Genoa-born graphic designer Di Genaro mainly deals with visual identity and editorial design. He used to collaborate with the financial newspaper Il Sole 24 Ore and is currently art directing Link magazine. Since 2008 he's taught as a visiting professor at IUAV San Marino and Bauer cfp Milano.

Ilaria Tomat: Ilaria moved to Milan to study and work as a graphic designer. While working in Milan she had the chance to collaborate with 46xy graphic design studio and with magazines such as "Abitare," "IL" and the leading financial newspaper Il Sole 24 Ore. She's now working as a senior graphic designer at studio FM milano.
http://davidedigennaro.com/
http://cargocollective.com/ilariatomat

DOPLUDÓ COLLECTIVE *P056-059*

Dopludó Collective was found in 2006 at St. Petersburg. The word "Dopludó" means "two plus two" in English. They apply this name to the absurd mathematical formula "2+2=5," which has been proved several times and has served as a potential key to reconsider all mathematics from the beginning.
The team enjoys working with the mystical and mythological images and more or less abstract content. Together they work on illustrations, objects, installations, interiors and public projects worldwide.
www.dopludo.com

DUANE DALTON *P092-095; P170-171*

Dalton, a graphic designer and artist from Dublin, Ireland, currently lives in London, where he works as a designer at SEA Design. He studied at The Institute of Art, Design and Technology (IADT).
Dalton specializes in the following areas of graphic design: identity, logo design, print, editorial / layout, album artwork, poster design and photography. He is passionate about minimal and reductive design qualities that communicate a clear and precise message. This attribute is common throughout the majority of his work.
www.duanedalton.com

EUGÉNIE GARCIA *P106-109*

After successfully completing a master's degree in graphic design, Eugénie chose to focus on every printable media. Her work centers on the idea of "realness." Her eyes sharpened to colors, she strengthened her work with invigorating and perceptible chromatic propositions. Later, she went to the Netherlands, which enabled her to practice graphic design without boundaries. At the age of twenty-four, she extended her creativity further and began to work with textiles. She shares her vision of the fashion industry through her brand, Epolet.
www.eugeniegarcia.com / www.epolet.fr

EPIFORMA *P148-149*

Epiforma is a multidisciplinary design studio established in 2014 that creates a diverse range of visual stories across multiple disciplines. Combining together a love for narrative and strategy that influences experimentalism and functionality, they build systems to generate creative outputs that define an innovative experience between clients and their audience.
http://www.epiforma.com/

FFURIOUS *P167*

Born from the desire to collaborate and grow with like-minds in creative design, fFurious began with the simple belief that only with good people can there be good work, and only with good work can a collective such as fFurious thrive.
Today, fFurious is a multi-disciplinary creative agency, thanks in part to an enthusiastic group of clients that includes advertising agencies, publishing companies, and small businesses, as well as MNCs, non-profit organizations and government bodies.
http://www.ffurious.com

FREDIC BARRERA *P206-207*

Fredic Barrera is a graphic designer who recently completed his university studies in Barcelona. He considers himself a curious and demanding person, in favor of experimentation and finding surprising solutions on his projects, and is always transmitting ideas through graphic language. He likes to work on identity projects that allow him to provide value and identification to a project, and is constantly seeking new sources of inspiration.
www.behance.net/fredicbarrera

GARBETT DESIGN *P130-131; P232*

Garbett Design (formerly Naughtyfish) is an established design studio based in Sydney, focusing on excellence in brand identity and delivering extraordinary creative outcomes for clients in a wide range of sectors.
http://garbett.com.au/

GHOST *P166*

Ghost Design is a multidisciplinary design studio specializing in visual identities, web development and product design. The design studio is run by passionate craftsmen, who strive to create vivid, rich and functional solutions. They work for clients who appreciate creative, practical ideas and enjoy direct interaction with designers.They offer high-end designs at competitive prices. Ghost Design strives for continuous interaction between the client and designer from the project's start to the delivery.
http://www.ghost.no/

GLAD CREATIVE *P211*

Glad is a small contemporary branding and design agency based in Durham, North East England. Established in 2011, the company's profile has risen quickly and brought opportunities to work for clients such as Tesco, V&A, Alvarez and Amazon. The studio is characterized by a commitment to ideas and a love for negative space, flexible branding systems, and letterpress printing. In 2014, Glad was ranked #32 in the Design Week Creative Survey.
http://www.weareglad.com/

HERE DESIGN *P172-173*

Here Design is a small team of multi-disciplinary designers based in East London. The studio was set up in December 2005 by Kate Marlow, Caz Hildebrand and Mark Paton. Since then they have been crafting quietly powerful design for a client list of individuals, brands, charities and institutions that they believe in wholeheartedly.
Their collective experience includes design and strategic thinking for branding, packaging, print, publishing, point-of-sale, products and websites. This scope allows them to create effective and original solutions to work across any media.
http://www.heredesign.co.uk/

HEY STUDIO *P111; P144; P153*

Hey is a multidisciplinary design studio based in Barcelona, Spain, specializing in brand management and editorial design, packaging and interactive design.
They share the profound conviction that good design means combining content, functionality, graphical expression and strategy. As a result, their clients are offered personal service based on mutual understanding and trust, work focused on rational innovation, and advice directed to meet actual needs.
http://heystudio.es

HOUSE OF SL *P088-089*

House of SL is Steven Larkin, a graphic designer with experience in print, editorial, branding/identity and web design. He lives in London, England, and hopes one day to own a trio of Shiba Inus that will go to work with him at his own design agency.
www.house-of-sl.co.uk

INÊS CASTRO *P046-047*

Born in Portugal in 1992 and graduated in Communication Design from the Matosinhos School of Art and Design, Inês Castro currently works as a freelance designer and illustrator. As a graphic designer, she is inspired by basic elements and plain colors, and her visual imagery emerges from the deconstruction of itself. As an illustrator she works with details, textures and improvisation, developing work tending to critical thinking: different aesthetic lines in different work processes, serving different purposes and settings but that sometimes run together.
www.cargocollective.com/inescastro

JASON BOOTH *P142-143*

Jason Booth is a graphic designer and illustrator based in the UK. His main focus is publication design, typography, screen-printing and illustration, but he feels the designer's need to be multi-disciplinary, so an open mind and a willingness to learn new things are things he always employs.
His design work is an on-going process of finding himself as a designer and expressing that to craft original and tailored ideas and projects, with emphasis on clarity and efficiency.
www.helloyoungfriends.com

JULES TARDY *P194-197*

Jules Tardy is a multidisciplinary graphic designer and art director. After spending a few years working in London, Jules moved to New York, where he earned his master's degree from the School of Visual Arts in 2011. His work has since been recognized by leading design organizations and publishers such as the Type Directors Club and Eye Magazine. His projects include a wide range of clientele, from independent art galleries to industry leaders such as Google, Microsoft, 1 Hotel and Conde Nast. Jules is currently based in Brooklyn, New York.
http://julestardy.com/

KIMBERLY CORDEIRO; MARCUS LEE *P150-151*

Kimberly Cordeiro is a Singapore-based graphic designer who seeks to form exciting visual languages through experimentation and research. She draws inspiration from modern architecture and tries to imbue her designs with a sense of playfulness. Her approach focuses on breaking down complex ideas into simple images that can be easily understood by the layperson.

Marcus Lee is a graphic designer who operates out of Singapore. One of his specializations is creating highly detailed illustrations that draw inspiration from both street art and Asian cultures. He is passionate about working with different individuals and media to craft out intriguing design responses with a personal touch.
https://www.behance.net/kimberlycordeiro
https://www.behance.net/adoptyourmarcus

KROGH STUDIO *P228-229*

Copenhagen-based graphic designer and artist Kristina Krogh graduated as a graphic designer from the Graphic Arts Institute of Denmark in 2011. Fascinated by different materials and their surfaces, she believes the strong mix of both exclusive and cheap textual materials creates an interesting and unexpected combination. She is inspired by the everyday things and objects that surrounds her. Besides art she works as a freelance graphic designer.
www.kkrough.dk

KYRU NISA *P145*

Kyru Nisa is a Singaporean designer and a 3rd year student pursuing a Bachelor's Degree of Fine Arts, majoring in Visual Communication. She specializes in identity design, print and graphic design, and visual merchandising, and has an interest that covers a wide range design disciplines. Design is her forte; it's nothing serious but it's also nothing simple. She doesn't think of herself as a designer, but as a deliverer of ideas. To her, experimenting with design is the key to boosting one's talents.
http://kyrunisa.weebly.com

LAVA *P076-077*

Lava is an Amsterdam based design agency, founded in 1990. They have strong roots in editorial design, which has trained them to work as visual storytellers. Over the years, this way of thinking has lead to a unique approach to identity and communication design.
Lava's creative team consists of graphic, motion and interactive designers that work for a diverse range of clients from the commercial, governmental, non-profit and cultural sectors.
www.lava.nl

LEO PORTO *P222-225*

Leo Porto is a 21-year old graphic designer from Brazil who is currently attending the School of Visual Arts in New York City.
http://leoporto.com/

LIU YUAN *P110*

Liu Yuan is a Chinese graphic designer based at Shanghai.

LUIS FABRA *P070-073*

Luis Fabra has had extensive working experience as a graphic designer in different countries and cities. Since 2012, he has embraced the challenge of giving lectures for Visual Communications in different campuses across South East Asia.
He has experience in working in independent and international agencies, creating and executing global projects for brands like Pond's, GSK, Qatar Airways, and British Council, among others.
His work is focused in the fields of communication strategy, branding, graphic environments, digital advertising, print production, and typography.
http://cargocollective.com/lpfabra

MAINSTUDIO *P096-097*

Mainstudio is an Amsterdam based graphic design studio, founded by Edwin van Gelder in 2005. The studio creates projects deriving from the intersection of art, architecture and fashion, including publications, digital media and visual identities. Each project is characterized by a content driven editorial approach, led by typography, creating a synthesis of form and content. The studio embeds inventive printing techniques within traditional media, and explores innovative interaction design within its digital media output. An imaginative approach to art direction forms the essential foundation of the studio.
www.mainstudio.com

MARCEL HÄUSLER *P028-031; P233*

Marcel Häusler is an independent graphic designer based in Hamburg. His unique typographic style of work is related to subjects like corporate design, book and catalogue design, editorial design, exhibition design and posters.
He graduated as an honored Bachelor of Arts and has working experience for MAGMA Brand Design and EIGA Design, as well as several well-known museums. His work has been well-acknowledged by others.
Marcel writes for the German design blog SLANTED and is part of the mood image feed blog DailyInput.org. In 2012 he initiated, designed and moderated the type design conference "TYPO TALK – talks on type" at the Gutenberg-Museum Mainz. He also founded the research project called "TFA – Type Foundries Archive," which is an online platform listing type foundries worldwide.
www.marcelhaeusler.de

MARIANA SABATTINI *P118-121*

Mariana Sabattini was born in Bahia Blanca, Argentina, in 1990. In 2009 she moved to Buenos Aires to get a degree in Graphic Design in Faculty of Architecture, Design and Urbanism of the University of Buenos Aires, where she currently continues her training. Since 2006, she has worked in graphic design and illustration for various media.
www.marianasabattini.blogspot.com

MARGOT MADRANGES *P220-221*

Located in the city of Bordeaux, FLAT226 is an association which develops video games. In 2013 it consisted of the three founding members: Yannick Jouneau (3D Animator), Margot Madranges (2D Graphic Designer) and Marc Tranchant (Game Designer). The team independently develops their own projects and provides training on their premises and workshops at local schools. Except for some travelling and a sabbatical year in London, Margot Madranges has always lived in Bordeaux, where she studied Fine Arts and Graphic Design. She has a passion for Contemporary Art and uncluttered designs.
https://www.behance.net/Ginger_Kandy

MARTA GAWIN *P048-051*

Marta Gawin (born in 1985, Poland) is a multidisciplinary graphic designer specialized in visual identity, sign system, poster, information, exhibition and editorial design. Since achieving her MA in Graphic Design (Academy of Fine Arts, Katowice) in 2011, she has been working as a freelancer for cultural institutions and commercial organizations. Her design approach is conceptual, logical and content-driven. She treats graphic design as a field of visual research and formal experiments.
http://www.martagawin.com

MASQUESPACIO *P016-019*

Masquespacio is a creative consultancy that designs new experiences for brands and their customers through intelligent and creative tools for communication. The design firm, led by Ana Milena Hernández Palacios, has been recognized internationally for their innovative and unique interior design and branding projects.
http://www.masquespacio.com

MATHIEU HUBERT *P074-075*

Mathieu Hubert is a French art director/designer. He has lived abroad in Canada and the UK. His span of works ranges from art galleries and theaters to nationwide brands. When he doesn't work for others, he makes pictures, installations and objects under his personal brand, LM1M.
www.mathieuhubert.com / www. laissezmoiunmessage.com (LM1M)

MAURIZIO PAGNOZZI *P202-203*

Italian designer Maurizio Pagnozzi graduated from ILAS of Naples where he studied art direction and copywriting with full marks with honors. After graduation, he established a young advertising agency with Cristiano Vicedomini and Denise Di Nardo. Later he returned to Benevento to work as a teacher of visual communication. Teaching supports the freelance activities at his studio One Design. He works for clients who appreciate his direct style, which is clean and essential without being devoid of meaning or contents. He specializes in branding, corporate identity

and naming and packaging, with an aim to create works that combine concepts with strong functional and solid executions. In 2013 he won the Cread Portfolio Awards.
www.mauriziopagnozzi.com

MOUSEGRAPHICS *P134-135*

Design is an endless exercise in communication. Mousegraphics is a creative office that has worked under this principle since 1984, and has earned a longstanding success with it.
With a creative team currently consisting of seven designers, Mousegraphics works together with its clients as much in the development of full strategic proposals and plans as in the realization of targeted, partial applications. Moreover, it has been internationally acknowledged with a plethora of awards and publications which help the agency excellent in all related levels of communications. Mousegraphics is also a member of both EDEE and Design Lobby.
www.mousegraphics.gr

MURMURE *P174-177*

Murmure creative agency was started in Caen in 2010 and specializes in strong visual identities in fields such as arts, culture, music and luxury.
The agency is led by two artistic directors (Julien Alirol and Paul Ressencourt) and aspires to produce and develop singular creative and aesthetic projects adapted to its clients' desires. Murmure is a multi-faceted platform able to adapt its size and aptitudes due to a wide network of multidisciplinary collaborators who are at the cutting edge of their own fields.
www.murmure.me

MY NAME IS WENDY *P084-085; P086-087*

My Name is Wendy was born in 2006 from the collaboration of two independent graphic designers, Carole Gautier and Eugénie Favre. This collaboration unites expertise in graphic and plastic art. The group produces visual identities, typefaces, formal principals, pictures, patterns and printings. They feel that a project is first of all an encounter gathering competences and mutual ethics. The group also produces a limited number of posters and can use different platforms within plastic realizations to satisfy its needs for expression.
http://www.mynameiswendy.fr/

OPISSO *P210*

Opisso Studio specializes in branding strategies, graphic design and interactive communication. With more than 15 years of experience, they have successfully implemented many brand and communication projects with passion and talent.
The main objective is to collaborate with brands in order to enable them to build long-lasting relationships with their users, consumers, and clients, and to communicate

with them in the best way possible, regardless of channel.
http://opissostudio.com/

PACO GRACIA TEROL *P169*

Paco Gracia Terol is a Spanish graphic designer and creative who is passionate about all forms of art. He finished his studies in May 2014 at the School of Arts and Design, Alicante. Spontaneous, daring, and happy as can be, he always looks to improve new ideas and be as creative as possible. He loves mixing manual and digital techniques and enjoys playing with colors in his designs. He currently works as a freelance graphic designer.
www.mrthankiu.com

PETE TONG *P024-025*

Pete, @ HEYPETETONG, is a graphic and motion designer based in Singapore. He is currently pursuing a Degree in Fine Arts (Visual Communication) in Nanyang Technological University.
Pete is a strong believer that form should follow function. While a design may look pretty, it should have a vital primary purpose to fulfill. In all of his work, Pete seeks to delve into a deeper understanding of the given assignment to provide solutions that exceed mere form and are rooted in long-term functionality.
http://cargocollective.com/heypetetong

QUIM MARIN *P104-105*

Quim Marin is a designer based in Barcelona, Spain, whose penchant for modernist Swiss design can be seen clearly throughout his portfolio of work. He loves type and color blocking.
www.quimmarin.com

RAW COLOR *P184-187; P192-193*

The work of Raw Color reflects a sophisticated treatment of material and color through the mixing of the fields of graphic design and photography. This aesthetic is reflected through the research and experiments used to build their visual language. Daniera ter Haar & Christoph Brach work on self initiated and commissioned projects in their Eindhoven based studio.
www.rawcolor.nl

RAY YEN *P208-209*

Ray Yen was born in Taipei, Taiwan. He majored in commercial design at Chung Yuan Christian University. He is currently a freelance graphic designer, specializing in brand, corporate identity design and typography design, and packaging design.
www.behance.net/rayyen

REJANE DAL BELLO *P012-015*

Senior Graphic Designer & Illustrator Rejane Dal Bello has been based in London since 2012. Originally from Rio de Janeiro, she began her career working for renowned branding and design companies in Brazil. After receiving her BA in graphic design in Rio de Janeiro, Rejane was educated under Milton Glaser in New York. She completed her MA at Post in the Netherlands in 2006. During her MA, Rejane started her 8-year serving for Studio Dumbar, which has established a unique position in Dutch design. Meanwhile she has taught graphic design and creative process at St Joost Art School.
Rejane is currently a senior designer at Wolff Olins, a well-known and established brand consultancy that specializes in developing brand experiences, creatively-led business strategies and visual identities.
http://rejanedalbello.com/

RM&CO *P154-157*

RM&CO, founded in 2013 by Pete Rossi and Alfio Mazzei, is an independent, multi-disciplinary graphic design, visual communication and branding consultancy with studios based in Glasgow, London and Balerna, Switzerland. RM&CO have been awarded and recognized by ADC, D&AD, Graphis and Red Dot. They believe in ideas and socially engaging work coupled with a simple philosophy based on intelligent, well-crafted and original design that makes a difference and solves problems effectively. Their work is informed by the process and development inherent within any one given project, driven by ideas and not relying on aesthetics and style. They are firm believers in pushing boundaries, but their meticulous approach, based on research, process, and development, allows them to serve their client's purpose with passion, detail, dedication and love to find the relevant solutions to a wide variety of projects and commissions. They also collaborate with a wide variety of specialized and skilled freelance designers, writers, illustrators, motion designers, photographers and programmers who excel at their respective disciplines.
www.rossimazzei.com

ROBERT LOMAS & JAMES HAYES *P140-141*

Robert Lomas is a brew-powered designer and image maker from Manchester. He spends his days working across digital design and branding at Design By Day, and explores his love of typography, color and geometry through screen printing in his spare time.

James Hayes is a graphic designer with a keen eye for tangible graphics and a big love for typography and illustration. He is a senior creative at a fashion wear company, using photography, digital illustration, and typography daily to create seasonal compositions and layouts for all types of online, interactive, and printed marketing.
www.lomasdesign.co.uk
www.james-hayes.co.uk

ROCKET & WINK *P098-101*

Rocket & Wink. Since May 2011, Rocket Man and Nature Boy have been a team. And they see themselves as more than just some condiments a waiter sat at an empty breakfast buffet. They dish up projects in all categories—design, illustration, literature, product development and conception, and they always move at full throttle.
For clients who appreciate the gentle vibrations of a hazelnut-sized colibri-collecting nectar at a Giant Lobelia just as much as the colossal burp of a mammoth that's just demolished a greasy repast from the Elvis cookbook.
http://www.rocketandwink.com/

ROSETA Y OIHANA *P036-037;P112-113; P136-137*

Roseta y Oihana is a graphic design studio created in 2010 by Roseta Mus Pons and Oihana Herrera Erneta, with offices in Barcelona and Pamplona. Roseta y Oihana not only specializes in sign design, but also VI, publications, webs, exhibitions and posters. By working closely with clients and devoting their full team to projects, the studio well serves their clients' needs, who include several renowned Spanish institutions and organizations. Their works are widely-published and exhibited, among which "Helvetica. A new typeface?" at Design Hub Barcelona is highlighted.
www.rosetayoihana.com

ROYAL STUDIO *P212-213*

The Royal Studio is a fierce Portuguese studio with a strong emphasis in the competitive world. Grown in Oporto, and influenced by the avid game-playing in the typography-filled streets, their approach has a solid base in the realm of communications, enabling them to develop design solutions that entwine themselves with other graphic actions. Originality is key in all of their work, which focuses on the creation of unique client-led identities for products and services. Conscious, wise and impactful, the studio's true master is their drive to provide every client with the unique Royal touch.
www.theroyalstudio.com

SAFFRON *P218-219*

Saffron was established in 2001 with a simple but compelling vision: to build a strong brand consultancy that utilizes both strategic thinking and creativity. Since then, Saffron has helped transform brands and businesses with the clarity of their rigorous thinking and the courage of their bold ideas. On this basis, Saffron mixes rational, evidence-based analysis and intuitive, judgment-based understanding to meet their clients' varied needs with creative thinking and tailored techniques of brand strategy, brand expression and brand experience.
Saffron has deliberately built a global business that operates as one seamless company across all of their offices.
http://saffron-consultants.com

SALMA SHAMEL *P102-103*

Salma Shamel is an Egypt-based graphic designer, specialized in identities, packaging, print and publication design.
https://www.behance.net/salmashamel

SOLID *P066-067*

Solid is a creative consulting agency that focuses on developing and managing visual identity systems and offering innovative web solutions for clients. They specialize in visual identities and brand design, in the planning of successful advertising campaigns, and the development of innovative websites and web applications.
www.solidstudio.it

SOULCRAFT *P230-231*

Soulcraft is a Curitiba based creative office, delivering creative multidisciplinary solutions for all kinds of clients; big and small brands, professionals, artists and more.
www.soulcraft.com.br

STAHL R *P078-079; P080-083*

Stahl R, a Berlin based internationally-recognized design studio, was founded in 2012 by Tobias Röttger and Susanne Stahl. It offers unique design solutions for a broad range of clients from both commercial and cultural fields and provides a diverse range of design disciplines: from visual identities, publication design environmental design, editorial and art direction, to time-based media and digital projects. Driven by both research and concept, Stahl R believes in a project-specific approach that leads to thoughtful, intelligent and innovative work. The studio is a dynamic system in scope and scale, strengthened by a network of talented creatives from all disciplines.
www.stahl-r.com

STUDIO ANOTHER DAY *P158-161*

Studio Another Day is the graphic design studio of Yorick de Vries, who offers a strong visual language that speaks with its audience. Together with Bart Van Haren, a conceptual, systematical designer with a passion for the public domain, Studio Another Day both provides free inspiring forms while creating designs that can bridge the distance between two extremes.
Another Day focuses on art and culture with a specialization on typography and printed matter. They enjoy creating images by hand, and crafting original materials for small and big time clients.
www.studioanotherday.nl

STUDIO NAAM *P038-039*

Established in 2011 in Utrecht, Studio Naam is a young design consultancy specializing in visual communication, graphic design for print and web, art direction, brand identity and typography. Naam believes that a well crafted and research-based process, led by "out of the box" ideas and inspirations, will translate into an intelligent visual solution that adds real value to visual products.
www.studionaam.com

TIM HUTCHINSON *P114-117*

Tim Hutchinson trained at St. Martins School of Art and earned an MA at the London Royal College of Art. Following this he co-founded Bark Design and and served as creative director for 15 years, working for a diverse range of clients.
He has recently set up an independent design practice to continue producing high quality, integrated design solutions for corporate identity, editorial, PR and marketing, exhibition and digital applications with the aim to aim to deliver bespoke, innovative, crafted and appropriate work. His work has been internationally published and he has given speeches at many top universities and colleges.
www.timhutchdesign.com

TGIF *P040-043*

TGIF is a Hong Kong based graphic design and branding studio. They believe that creative thinking brings out positive energy and provoking solutions for clients. They provide a full range of design services including branding, corporate communications, web-site design, marketing materials, packaging, exhibition and event design.
www.tgif.com.hk

TRAPPED IN SUBURBIA *P032-035, P122-123*

"Tell me and I'll forget; show me and I may remember; involve me and I'll understand." Trapped in Suburbia focuses on human interaction and engaging their audience. They don't expect them to sit back and relax; instead they take them on a graphic journey and surprise them.
www.trappedinsuburbia.com

VIRGINIA POL & ALBERT GOMEZ *P052-055*

Virginia Pol is a Barcelona based designer graduated from Eina, University Center of Design and Art, and holds a master's from Elisava School of Design and Engineering in Barcelona. She is currently working for Domo-a.

Albert Gomez Porta is a Barcelona based designer. He holds a master's degree from Elisava School of Design and Engineering and Barcelona, and has rich experience working as a designer. He currently works for Mucho.
https://www.behance.net/virginia_pol;
https://www.behance.net/albertgporta

VLADIMIR SHLYGIN *P204-205*

Vladimir Shlygin is graphic and interaction designer from Moscow. He started his design career when he was 16 at Art Lebedev studio. Since then he has mostly worked as a freelance designer, but will occasionally take on roles as an art director.
www.behance.net/vladimirshlygin

WERKLIG *P020-023*

Werklig is an independent brand design agency founded in 2008. The office is located in Helsinki, but they serve more than 50 clients both in Finland and internationally. They are designers, creatives and consultants—but most of all, they are problem solvers.
http://www.werklig.com/

ACKNOWLEDGEMENTS

We would like to express our gratitude to all of the designers and companies for their generous contribution of images, ideas, and concepts. We are also very grateful to many other people whose names do not appear in the credits but who made specific contributions and provided support. Without them, the successful completion of this book would not be possible. Special thanks to all of the contributors for sharing their innovation and creativity with all of our readers around the world. Our editorial team includes editor Javier Zheng and book designer Danni Song, to whom we are truly grateful.